17

small garden planner

small garden planner

Roger Sweetinburgh

CHANCELLOR
PRESS

SMALL GARDEN PLANNER

Editor Emily Wright
Executive Art Editor Mark Richardson
Designed by Bobby Birchall, Town Group Consultancy Ltd
Picture Research Sally Claxton
Production Controller Melanie Frantz

First published in Great Britain in 1995 by Hamlyn
a division of Octopus Publishing Group Ltd

This 2002 edition published by Chancellor Press,
an imprint of Bounty Books, a division of
Octopus Publishing Group,
2-4 Heron Quays, London E14 4JP

Copyright © 1995 Octopus Publishing Group Ltd
Reprinted 2003, 2004 (twice)

ISBN 0 7537 0518 4

A CIP catalogue record for this book is available from the British
Library

Printed in China

Contents

Designing your garden

Steps, walls, paths, a lawn and of course planting are just some of the features which help to produce an interesting garden.

Designing your garden

STARTING ON PAPER

No matter how small your garden is, it can always be made into a place for you to enjoy. Small gardens do, however, need very careful planning if they are to be a success, simply because so much has to be fitted in to such a small area.

The starting point for any design project is to draw a scaled plan of the area. This must show the house, boundaries and any other existing features or plants that are too permanent to move, or that you wish to retain. Plants or features that you do not want in your new design should be excluded from the scaled plan.

Measuring the garden

For an accurate, working scale drawing, you will need to measure your garden in some detail. Enter these measurements on a couple of preliminary sketch plans first, before using them to produce the scale drawing. The preliminary sketches must bear some resemblance to your plot, although they do not have to be to scale, and, if your site is very detailed and there is a great deal to record, you may well find it easier to make a large number of sketches. A separate sketch of just the

Measuring your garden

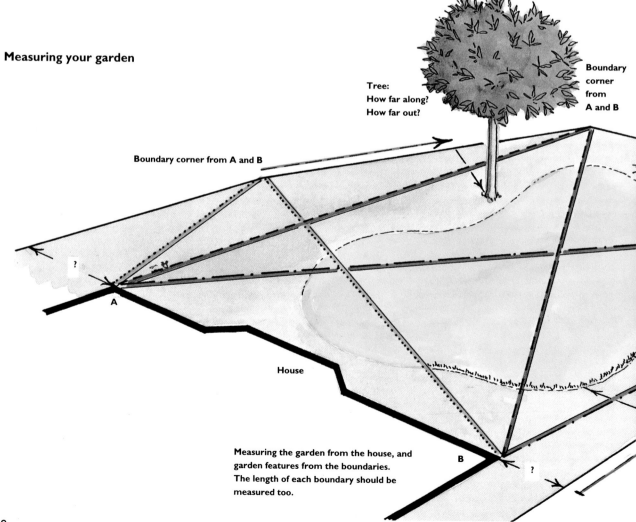

Tree:
How far along?
How far out?

Boundary corner from A and B

Boundary corner from A and B

?

A

House

Measuring the garden from the house, and garden features from the boundaries. The length of each boundary should be measured too.

B

?

Measuring your house and all its features

Beginning of the tape

Drain

Window

Bay window

Do not forget to measure the depth of the bay, the step and the height of the window sill from the ground

Drain:
How far out from the house?
How far along?

Step/door

Corner

It is important to measure as accurately as possible and to keep your measuring tape straight and tight. If objects or features are in the way, place your tape as close to them as you can.

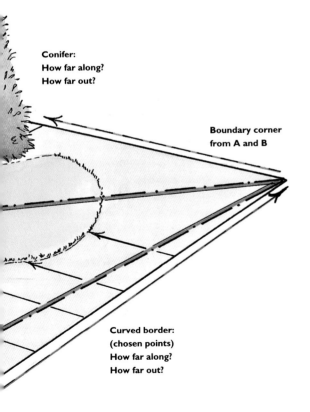

Conifer:
How far along?
How far out?

Boundary corner from A and B

Curved border:
(chosen points)
How far along?
How far out?

Plan how you are going to work your way around the garden so that you can be sure nothing will be left out. In a small area, much of the garden will be within reach of the house.

house, for example, will give you plenty of room to record doors, windows and drain pipes, all of which must be taken into account if you are going to do a really good design job.

Starting with the house, carefully measure and record the length of the walls, the position of doors and downstairs windows, along with other house-related features such as drains; drain covers must be measured to their centre and sketched at the appropriate angle. Next, measure and record the length of each different boundary.

Very few plots are actually square, and it is quite possible that some of your boundaries are not straight but change direction more than once. Rather than trying to record all the corners in relation to each other, it is much easier to plot them in relation to two fixed points, such as the corners of the house. This then places every change of direction and corner at the point of a triangle. Garden features and plants can then be plotted off their nearest boundary. Measure how far along and how far out at right angles the object is to the boundary and enter the measurement onto the sketch plan. For objects like a shed or greenhouse, measure two adjacent corners to get the position and angle of the building and then the overall dimensions to complete it. To plot curves off a straight line, use a series of how-far-along, how-far-out measurements. Finally, it is also a good idea to record the size of tree canopies and the diameter or width of shrubs.

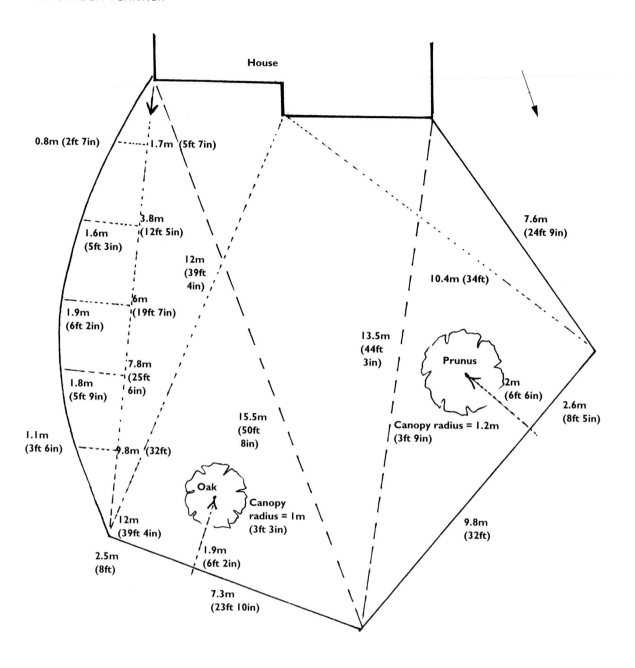

House

0.8m (2ft 7in)   1.7m (5ft 7in)

3.8m
(12ft 5in)

1.6m
(5ft 3in)

12m
(39ft
4in)

6m
(19ft 7in)

1.9m
(6ft 2in)

7.8m
(25ft
6in)

1.8m
(5ft 9in)

1.1m
(3ft 6in)

9.8m (32ft)

12m
(39ft 4in)

2.5m
(8ft)

15.5m
(50ft
8in)

Oak

Canopy
radius = 1m
(3ft 3in)

1.9m
(6ft 2in)

7.3m
(23ft 10in)

7.6m
(24ft 9in)

10.4m (34ft)

13.5m
(44ft
3in)

Prunus

2m
(6ft 6in)

Canopy radius = 1.2m
(3ft 9in)

2.6m
(8ft 5in)

9.8m
(32ft)

This shows how your measurements should be recorded on a rough sketch: clearly and uncluttered (but not to scale). Rather than overload a sketch like this, use canopies and note if any neighbouring trees overhang the boundary. Do not, however, measure any feature which you have no intention of keeping, but make a list of anything you intend to remove and re-use in a different position later.

Making a scale plan

The most useful scale to work to is 1 or 2cm to 1m (¼ or ⅛in to 1ft), depending on how big your garden is and the size of the paper you are using. It is easier to work on plain rather than graph paper so that you are not tempted to draw everything using a straight line and at right angles.

First draw the house. Next, plot the various boundary corners, using a pair of compasses for accuracy. Take the measurement between one house corner and one boundary corner, scale this down and set your

Measuring a slope

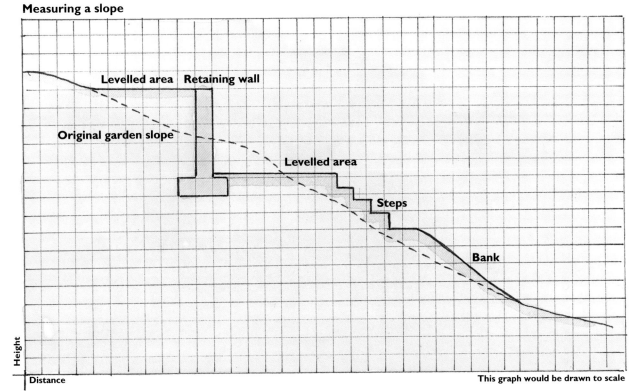

Levelled area | Retaining wall

Original garden slope

Levelled area

Steps

Bank

Height

Distance

This graph would be drawn to scale

A graph of ground heights to show the slope of a garden and what might be done with it.

compasses (that is to say, the length between the compass point and pencil point) to this length. On paper, place the point of the compass on the house corner and, pointing roughly in the direction of the boundary corner, draw a broad arc. Repeat the process, this time using the measurement between the second house corner and the same boundary corner. Where the two arcs meet is the apex of your boundary. Repeat this exercise until you have reproduced every corner then join them to produce the boundary. Check your drawing by measuring the distance from one boundary corner to the other and scaling it down; it should be the same as the equivalent distance on paper.

With the basic framework down on paper, you can now add other objects, using a set square for right angles, until you have an accurate plan of your plot.

Recording slopes

You can more or less ignore a very gently sloping garden, but any significant slopes should be measured and recorded. This will give you a cut-through section of all the changes of levels so you can plan features like walls, steps, terraces and banks. If your garden

slopes in two directions, you should record more than one line of measurements.

Use a straight length of wood (about 1.8m (6ft) long), a spirit level and a small steel tape measure. Fix the spirit level to the piece of wood so that it does not fall off.

Assuming that the incline is reasonably uniform across the garden, start at the top and place the end of the wood on the ground at the highest point and hold it level. Measure the gap (or drop) beneath the low end of the plank with the tape measure held as perpendicular as possible. Mark the point where the tape touches the ground and then move the opposite end of the wood downhill and place it on this mark to continue the series of measurements. Repeat this all the way down the centre of the slope until you have a line of measurements. Draw these up on graph paper as a section by starting at the top and drawing the horizontal measurements (the length of wood) and vertical drops to scale. You will end up with a section that looks rather like an uneven flight of steps and, if the bottom corners of each are joined up, the slope of the garden will appear.

Three basic styles of garden

A An example of a rectangular lay-out

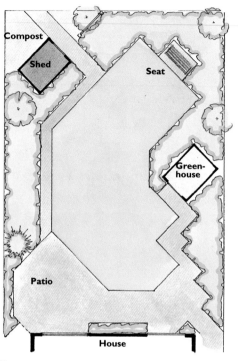

B An example of a diagonal lay-out

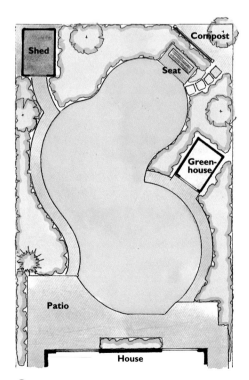

C An example of a circular lay-out

A This rectangular or formal approach will have many of its features symmetrically arranged, though not necessarily in equal proportions around the garden. Inevitably, some borders will be straight and narrow and the garden will have a high proportion of straight lines or predictable curves.

B Although this type of lay-out has straight lines, the built-in angle will offset features to produce a less predictable and formal effect. The likely result is a relatively modern garden rather than one which has an informal cottage-garden feel.

C This curving lay-out is a popular approach because it will produce an informal garden with some partially 'hidden' areas, places to walk and sit in, and borders of variable widths which can accommodate an attractive arrangement of plants.

THE NEW DESIGN

When designing a garden, first decide on the general theme you want, and then adapt it according to your lifestyle and various needs, such as a safe garden for small children. Make sure you do not go for anything too ambitious if you do not have the time to maintain it. Also, draw up a realistic budget and try to work within it.

Getting an overall feel for your garden will help you decide on these issues. Go outside at various times of the day and note the position of the sun, taking into account the shade cast by any neighbouring trees; think about where it might be comfortable to sit, where extra shelter or screening would be useful and which views or vistas, no matter how modest, have the potential to be developed. Do not forget that the garden must look good from several different vantage points, for example from windows, from garden benches and from the back door. Think about where the lawn should go, if you want paving or steps, and whether to include a water feature, rockery, pergola or decorative arch.

Choosing a theme

When choosing a theme, try to resist the temptation to line everything up in a series of parallel lines and instead explore creating more exciting shapes using diagonals and curves.

Most gardens are either designed to be rectangular, at 90° to the house, diagonally arranged from corner to corner or, more generally, circular and curved. This latter approach is very popular and most successful when based on a series of circles or arcs radiating out into the garden. Try to follow this theme through to all areas of the garden for as much continuity as possible. For example, a diagonal layout may look better if at least part of the patio is also diagonal, so that it all fits together. Similarly, a circular or curved layout may need at least one edge of the patio to be curved or angled so that it also locks into the shape of the lawn and borders.

Allocating space

A garden can be divided into three basic components: paving, lawn and border space and a successful garden design is a pleasing balance of these three areas. A sense of proportion is particularly important, otherwise you will end up with a tiny lawn swamped by an overpowering display of border plants, or a large expanse of paving dwarfing a tiny strip of flower bed. When planning a small garden, you should aim at dividing your space roughly into thirds, with an equal amount of paving, lawn and border. However, in a very small garden, grass is not always practical because it may wear out too quickly, and you may want to increase your paved area instead. Generally speaking, your border width should not be less than 45cm (18in) wide. It may help to mark out the outlines of the design with sand on the ground before coming to any final decision.

When allocating space, patios should be considered as part of the paving scheme. Make sure they are large

A circular lay-out

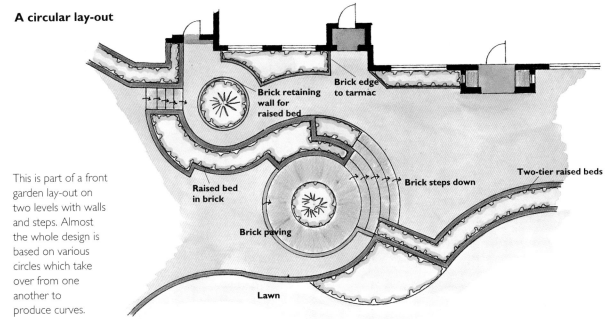

This is part of a front garden lay-out on two levels with walls and steps. Almost the whole design is based on various circles which take over from one another to produce curves.

Brick retaining wall for raised bed

Brick edge to tarmac

Raised bed in brick

Brick steps down

Two-tier raised beds

Brick paving

Lawn

Completing the design on paper

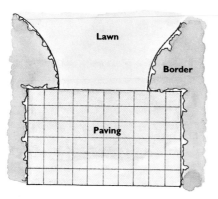

This arrangement tends to close in the patio, overpower it with planting and partly shut out the rest of the garden.

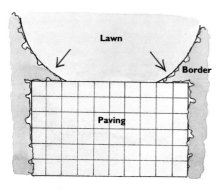

Here, a more open feel and better balance between lawn and paving has been achieved but with two awkward wedges of border.

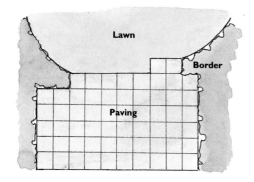

This lay-out is similar but the re-arranged paving has produced a slightly more interesting effect and eliminated the awkward wedges.

A modern garden

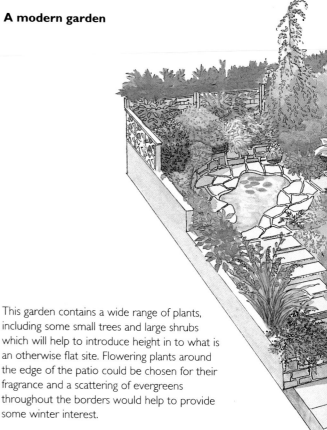

This garden contains a wide range of plants, including some small trees and large shrubs which will help to introduce height in to what is an otherwise flat site. Flowering plants around the edge of the patio could be chosen for their fragrance and a scattering of evergreens throughout the borders would help to provide some winter interest.

enough to accommodate a certain number of sun-loungers or tables and chairs. If possible, avoid hedges in favour of walls or fences which take up less space and provide support for a considerable range of flowering and highly ornamental climbing or wall plants. When it comes to paths, vary the width according to their intended use. A path from the pavement to the front door, for example, ought to be at least 90cm (3ft) wide, whereas one that is used less frequently could be as little as 45cm (18in) across. Arches, pergolas and other vertical structures should be at least 2.1m (7ft) high.

COMPLETING THE DESIGN ON PAPER

To transfer your ideas onto the scale plan, start by allocating the areas of lawn, paving and border and, when the overall shaping is more or less complete, start to slot in the garden features. Use a scale ruler constantly to keep everything in proportion and to avoid losing track of space, resulting in things being too large or, as is more often the case, too small.

INTRODUCING PLANTS

Only start thinking about plants once your basic design is finished. The plants you choose should suit the prevailing soil conditions of your garden. It is no good wanting to plant rhododendrons and other acid-loving plants if your soil is alkaline. Many of the most popular plants need a fairly open, sunny position, although it is surprising how many shade-loving shrubs and perennials exist.

You must also remember that every plant has a different shape and height and should be placed where it can naturally achieve this. However, if space is really restricted, a certain amount of pruning will help keep growth in control. When deciding how many plants (more particularly shrubs) will fit into a certain space, it can be helpful to envisage how large they might be in, say, five years time and plant accordingly. Perhaps after about ten years, some will need taking out or, at least, some drastic pruning. Small weeping trees and shrubs are sometimes difficult to plant around and need a relatively isolated and uncluttered space within a border, where they can develop and be appreciated as individual specimens.

Ornamental trees, conifers and large evergreen shrubs can be introduced to provide some strategic screening within the garden, a bit of height and perhaps some focal points as well. Screening provided by a dense row of fast-growing conifers, such as x *Cupressocyparis leylandii*, is quick and efficient but is very difficult to limit. It is often better to have a screen of mixed plants, including some conifers, which are also, as a group, less vigorous and, therefore, unlikely to outgrow the garden quite so quickly.

If your scale plan is large enough, you can sketch in the trees and conifers that you would like to plant eventually, along with large areas of shrubs and ornamentals. When it comes to making detailed planting plans, make individual scale plans using a scale of 2cm to 1m (¼in to 1ft) for each border. Make detailed notes on all these plans in order to identify and name all the plants within those groups. Different groups of plants such as herbs, roses and alpines, can be used as special features within a garden. If you are uncertain about the final choice of plants make notes in pencil so that you can change your mind later.

Garden plans

Seclusion, somewhere to sit in the sun and borders overflowing with colour and fragrance are some of the most important requirements in a garden.

Creating the illusion of space

A garden full of illusions

This garden displays a number of techniques which can be used to make it look longer or wider than it really is. Although much of this is done with structures, plants play an important part too.

Garden plan

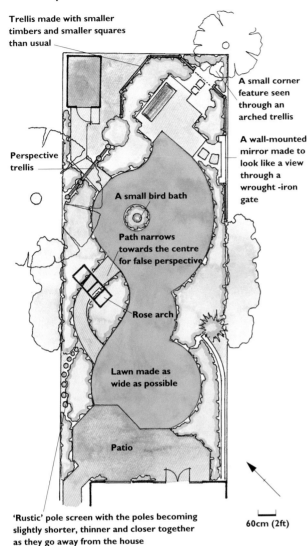

Trellis made with smaller timbers and smaller squares than usual

A small corner feature seen through an arched trellis

A wall-mounted mirror made to look like a view through a wrought-iron gate

Perspective trellis

A small bird bath

Path narrows towards the centre for false perspective

Rose arch

Lawn made as wide as possible

Patio

'Rustic' pole screen with the poles becoming slightly shorter, thinner and closer together as they go away from the house

60cm (2ft)

A combination of techniques, including false perspective, a cleverly positioned mirror and various screens all work together to produce an overall impression of length and spaciousness.

There are many ways of making something appear larger than it really is, especially indoors, but out in the garden this is much harder to achieve because of all the surrounding influences beyond your control. Making a garden seem larger can be interpreted in different ways; larger could mean longer and wider or it could mean 'more extensive', an effect that can be achieved by dividing up the garden space into smaller sections so that it takes longer to walk around – it is all a matter of creating an illusion.

All illusions have limitations so if you want to make something in the garden look further away than it

really is you must try to make sure that no other familiar objects or features nearby give the game away. This is why a collection of illusions, all working together, is more likely to fool the eye, at least for a while, into believing that the garden is more spacious than it really is. You might imagine that the most effective way of making the garden seem larger is to have 'wall-to-wall' grass and little else but there are, in fact, several very interesting techniques that can be used quite effectively depending on the specific effect you want to achieve.

Colour

The effects produced by certain colours can be usefully harnessed to create illusions of space. For example, any bright red or scarlet objects on a transparency held up to the light will appear to stand out in front of anything else pictured on it. Similarly, a room decorated with very busy, brightly-coloured wallpaper will seem much small than one of a similar size with plain white or pastel walls. If the planting at the far end of a garden contains a lot of red or orange flowers, these will have the effect of making that end of the garden seem closer – an illusion that may be useful in long narrow plots. The situation can, to some extent, be reversed by using very pale colours, especially blue, white and grey to make the boundaries of a small plot appear remote and indistinct.

The use of bright colours, particularly red and orange, in a distant border can help to make a long garden seem shorter than it really is.

Pale colours, especially blue, grey, white and light greens, can help to make a border appear more distant as well as cool and restful.

Pushing back the boundaries

The size of a plot is often judged by the position of its boundaries. If a neighbouring plot has tall dense shrubs just the other side of a boundary wall or fence, more shrubs could be planted in front of the near side so that the fence is completely surrounded by the planting and therefore, in effect, disappears. Once this has happened it will appear that the boundary must be on the far side of all these shrubs and not in the centre of them. The border in front of the fence would need to be at least 2m (6ft 6in) deep in order to produce the desired effect so this technique would only really be suitable in a medium-sized or large garden. In a small garden the extra planting needed would take up so much valuable space that it would be counter-productive.

Extensive carpets

Lawn and border shaping can contribute a great deal to the sense of space within the garden. This and the planting can easily be arranged to divide the garden up into distinct areas, or 'rooms'. In addition, any gaps linking one area with another should be kept as open as possible and the same surface should be used throughout. One example is grass, but if grass (or paving) cannot be seen flowing from one area to the other to unify the design the garden could appear smaller overall. The principle is the same as that in a house, which can appear larger if all the internal doors are kept wide open and the same colour carpet is used throughout than if the carpet is changed in some of the rooms or the doors are partially closed.

False Perspective

This is a technique which can be effective if used selectively and sensibly. It is based on the fact that parallel lines appear to converge as they get further away and objects appear smaller at a distance. A pair of hedges, although seemingly parallel, can be planted to converge slightly to give a false impression of distance. This can be further enhanced by making them slightly shorter towards their furthest end. Similarly, a garden path can be made to appear longer by constructing it to be slightly narrower towards the far end. This narrowing must never be overdone, however, since the eye is not easily fooled.

Another thing to consider is how these false perspectives would look if they were viewed from the

Dividing a garden into various areas can help to make it seem more extensive than it is, although overdoing this can have the opposite effect.

Looking back towards the house in the same garden

It is important that any false perspectives or other illusions are carefully planned and positioned so that they do not jar from the opposite viewpoint.

Broad sweeps of lawn are one of the easiest ways of creating a feeling of spaciousness.

opposite direction. In some cases they would look very odd and would possibly create the opposite impression to that which was intended they achieve. If this is the case, the effects should perhaps be used only in those situations where they could never be viewed from the opposite direction.

Perspective trellis

This is a flat, wall-mounted trellis, made from laths set into a main framework. In most designs, there is a central archway with lines radiating outwards, starting on the edge of the arch and finishing on the frame around the outside. Other laths are fixed vertically but at diminishing distances apart as they approach the edge of the central arch. This produces a 'tunnel' effect with the arch appearing to be at the far end whereas in fact the whole structure is flat on a wall. The illusion is helped if the area of wall within the arch is made as textureless as possible and perhaps painted a fairly dark colour. This would be more

successful than visible rows of bricks which would ruin the illusion straight away.

If there is planting space in front of the trellis then the arrangement of plants can also help emphasize the effect: use plants with progressively smaller leaves (or flowers) towards the rear. There are some groups of plants which are available in a variety of sizes: hebes, for example, cover a whole range of sizes and could be useful here, and ornamental grasses are also available in various sizes. In both these cases, the slightly taller and larger-leafed types would be used furthest from the wall trellis.

Mirrors and gates

Attention to detail is very important for all illusions. One of the most intriguing techniques for making a garden appear larger is to use mirrors. A particularly effective method is to create the impression of a garden gate by building a brick arch the size of a standard, wrought-iron gate onto (not in to) a brick wall. A moisture-resistant mirror, precisely the size of the arch aperture, is then fixed against the wall, inside the arch of brickwork. A wrought-iron gate is fixed on hinges within the arch so that it closes up tight against the mirror. When the mirror needs cleaning, the gate can be swung out of the way.

This whole feature must be positioned so that the viewer cannot see him or herself in it. The image will bounce off the mirror at 90° so, on a plan and using a set square, it should be possible to predict precisely what would be seen in the mirror at various angles and from different vantage points.

For a short time, of course, it will appear as if another garden lies beyond the gate, but the illusion will be spoilt if the feature is constructed on what is obviously a garage wall, for example. The ground at the bottom of the mirror and the gate should be mulched with stones or rocks so that falling rain is prevented from splashing mud over the lower half of the mirror and ruining the illusion. Some planting can also be introduced here and will look twice as much reflected in the mirror.

The mirror will have to be resistant to moisture, otherwise the silvering on the back could come off. Mirror glass is sometimes available which is already moisture resistant but, if not, can be made so by having the back painted over with gloss paint or varnish and 'all-weather' transparent tape applied very carefully and discreetly all round the edges to produce a weather-tight edge to the glass.

Island beds can help to break up large expanses of lawn and introduce added interest to a garden arrangement.

PLANTING FOR ILLUSIONS

A selection of plants with light-coloured leaves or flowers and vigorous shrubs can help create an illusion of space in your garden.

Agapanthus praecox* ssp. *orientalis
Perennial with large, dense umbels of sky-blue flowers in late summer.

***Cistus* x *laxus* 'Snow White'**
Smallish shrub producing a succession of freely borne white flowers in summer. Does best in light, well-drained soil.

Cistus x *laxus* 'Snow White'

Hydrangea macrophylla 'Madame A. Riverdin'

***Deutzia* x *magnifica* 'Staphyleoides'**
Vigorous, upright shrub with pure white blooms in early summer. Grows to height of 2.4m (8ft).

***Hydrangea* spp.**
Particularly blue or white-flowered varieties. Deciduous, woody shrubs producing heads of small flowers from mid- to late summer.

Jasminum polyanthum
(jasmine)
Evergreen, woody stemmed, twining climber with large clusters of fragrant white flowers from late summer to winter.

Nicotiana alata
(tobacco plant)
White-flowered, rosette-forming perennial, fragrant at night.

Philadelphus coronarius 'Aureus'

Spiraea japonica

Philadelphus coronarius
(mock orange)
Deciduous shrub with fragrant white flowers in late spring and early summer.

***Spiraea nipponica* 'Snowmound'**
Spreading shrub with dark green leaves and profuse, dense clusters of white flowers from mid-spring.

Working with short, wide spaces

A short, wide garden

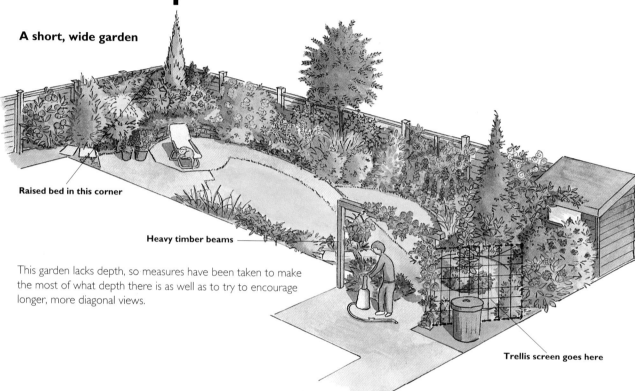

Raised bed in this corner

Heavy timber beams

This garden lacks depth, so measures have been taken to make the most of what depth there is as well as to try to encourage longer, more diagonal views.

Trellis screen goes here

Not all gardens are square or rectangular in shape. Some, while being a normal width across the back of the house, only extend a short distance out to produce a plot which is short and wide. Making a garden like this appear deeper and less wide than it really is can be very difficult, especially if there are some very dominant features that attract the eye just the other side of the boundary. There are, however, several ideas which might help.

Making the most of the space

In the garden illustrated overleaf, some of the conifers at one end of a tall hedge have been replaced by a small ornamental tree and a screen of 'rustic' poles covered with climbing plants. Other than these and a few shade- and drought-resistant plants against the hedge, the planting has been concentrated in those areas furthest away from the hedge because the back of the house is in full sun for most of the day.

It has been possible to include a few curves in the design but the hedge restricts the depth available so, on the whole, an angled lay-out has been adopted, with the patio and its paving set at an angle of about 45° to the house to draw the eye out towards the corner seat. The view from this seat would be quite pleasant because much of the planting has been concentrated across the back of the house. The bird bath would, once again, help to encourage a diagonal view. The small utility area at the far end of the house provides a brief opportunity to break away from the

A tripod or trellis of poles will provide height and somewhere for climbing plants without taking up a lot of space or casting too much shadow.

This vista, created by an arch and a seat, helps to add dimensions and visual interest to a relatively short, wide plot, making the most of the space available.

'short and wide' structure and creates a less claustrophobic atmosphere for anyone sitting on the seat.

The first garden illustrated on these pages, does not have the problem of a hedge and is, therefore, lighter. This has meant that planting can be more concentrated away from the house and can be viewed from indoors. Despite the shallowness of the plot, it has been possible to create a mainly curved lay-out with two reasonable areas of lawn.

The small circular corner patio, backed by a raised bed, acts as a diagonal focus and would be a pleasant place to sit out on a sunny day. From here, the small utility area at the end of the house is partly screened from view by the wooden rose arch and a trellis set at an angle which hides a compost bin. The small shed would waste space if it, too, was positioned at an angle in a small garden like this. The fact that it has been lined up with the fence is, to some extent, concealed by a conifer, some shrubs and a climber. The space between here and the utility area is partly devoted to a small circular bed containing a Ballerina fruit tree and some herbs.

Garden plan

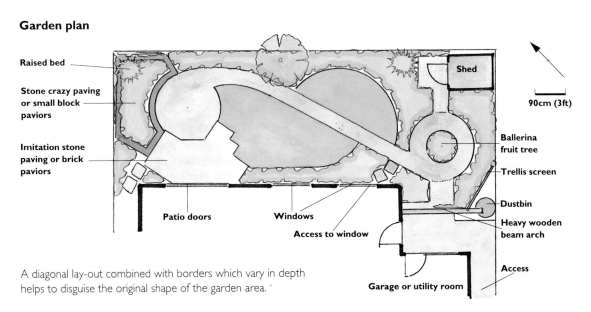

Raised bed

Stone crazy paving or small block paviors

Imitation stone paving or brick paviors

Patio doors

Windows

Access to window

Garage or utility room

Shed

90cm (3ft)

Ballerina fruit tree

Trellis screen

Dustbin

Heavy wooden beam arch

Access

A diagonal lay-out combined with borders which vary in depth helps to disguise the original shape of the garden area.

An alternative treatment

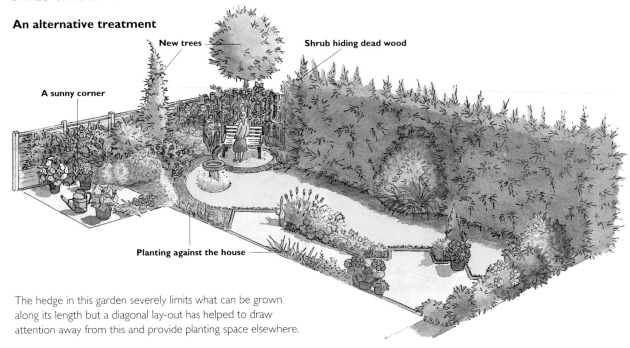

New trees

Shrub hiding dead wood

A sunny corner

Planting against the house

The hedge in this garden severely limits what can be grown along its length but a diagonal lay-out has helped to draw attention away from this and provide planting space elsewhere.

Dividing the garden into sections

Any space that has been divided up into several distinct areas will feel larger because it will take longer to walk through it and there is likely to be more of interest to see on the way. You can apply this technique to short, wide gardens although, paradoxically, it can

This raised bed provides some useful height in this garden and helps to lead the eye around a corner and away from the boundary.

make the garden seem less spacious overall because the individual area of each section is relatively small. To counteract this, you should incorporate a good broad path or route running right through the garden from one area to another, preferably all in the same material, as in the garden on the previous page. Paving or gravel are the most practical materials to use for hard areas throughout the sectioned-off garden with one larger, uncluttered area at least 2.7m (9 ft) across for a rotary washing line. A garden treated in this way is unlikely to have room for any effective lawn and so is probably unsuitable for young children.

In a short, wide garden, any division has to be done very carefully so as not to spoil or restrict the outlook from each window and door across the back of the house. On the other hand, done skilfully, it could provide each window with a different and interesting view and, rather than being all the same size or all parallel to the back of the house, the areas could be varied in both their size and aspect.

Probably the quickest and easiest way to create separate areas is to put up screens. There are many different types to choose from but your choice will probably be determined by the style of your garden. Woven panels of hazel (*Corylus*), willow (*Salix*) or heather are popular but quite dense. Split bamboo cane is light both in weight and in colour but not very durable, while reed screens start off as a similar pale yellow to split cane but are much thicker and stronger

Garden plan

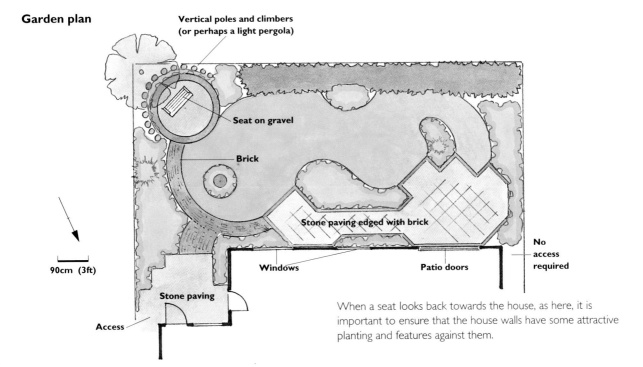

Vertical poles and climbers
(or perhaps a light pergola)

Seat on gravel

Brick

Stone paving edged with brick

No access required

90cm (3ft)

Windows

Patio doors

Stone paving

Access

When a seat looks back towards the house, as here, it is important to ensure that the house walls have some attractive planting and features against them.

and age to a darker colour. If dense materials are too overpowering, screen block walls or trellis could be used as a partial screen. You can even cut out 'windows' or apertures in trellis panels to establish a visual link between one area and the next.

Within each area, or 'room', the various features you introduce should be quite small and in proportion to their surroundings. These could include places to sit, water features, ornaments and a selection of relatively slow-growing plants which might be chosen for a particular theme – herbs, roses, herbaceous plants or even different colour themes. Any tall plants will have to be kept quite narrow because of the limited space but much of the height in the planting can come from climbing plants growing over the screens.

A more spacious lay-out

If the divided garden is inappropriate then a more open approach can be used to draw attention to the furthest corners – the longest possible distance away in a short and wide garden. This suggests a diagonal design with the overall lay-out, including all features and paths going diagonally across from one corner to the other rather like those illustrated here. For this to work, you will have to place inviting features in the furthest corners as focal points, for example, a pool, perhaps with a fountain which should be highly visible (and perhaps audible) from the house, a rock

feature, a sundial, a bird bath or a garden seat. The advantage of a seat is that, apart from being visually appealing in itself, it provides a vantage point from which the garden can be viewed in the opposite direction. It will, therefore, be important in such close surroundings, to make sure that the view from this seat is attractive and not merely a mass of ugly drain pipes and bare walls. A diagonal path that is curving or

Sometimes the paving within a circular lay-out can be designed to feature a large pot or some other ornamental feature. This provides variation and softens the visual effect of the paving.

An island bed could be used as a focal point in a diagonal layout, especially if hedges make normal planting difficult.

COMPACT, UPRIGHT SHRUBS FOR SCREENING

Here are some ideas for shrubs (excluding conifers) that stay relatively narrow and compact. Some will grow quite tall and need occasional pruning.

Berberis thunbergii 'Helmond Pillar'

Buxus (box)
Suitable only if clipped

Daphne mezereum and **D. odora f. alba**

Enkianthus campanulatus
Prefers a lime-free soil

Erica terminalis

Euonymus japonicus
All the available varieties are suitable

Olearia x haastii
Narrow at first. Attractive daisy-like flowers from mid- to late summer

Phlomis fruticosa
Whorls of golden-yellow flowers in summer

Phormium tenax
Bold, sword-shaped leaves

Rosmarinus officinalis 'Miss Jessopp's Upright'
An upright form of rosemary

Buxus sempervirens

Phormium tenax

heading straight for the corner features, the subsequent shaping of lawns and borders, and the strategic placing or angling of some screens, an arch or pergola can all help to emphasize the diagonal view and will help to discourage the shortest view, straight out from the back of the house.

Being overlooked

It is quite possible that this shortest view looks straight onto a neighbour's house or some eyesore which, because the garden is so narrow at this point, could be quite close. Any screening to block this view must be done especially carefully, because if the sun shines from that direction, anything too tall could cut out a lot of valuable light and actually be counter-productive in disguising the shape of your garden. A row of tall conifers, for example, would positively emphasize the short, wide shape of the garden and would be very hard to incorporate into any new design. Most conifers reach a width of about 75cm (2ft 6in) once they are tall enough to be an effective screen, and would therefore use up valuable space just where it is most needed.

A better solution would be to increase the fence height with some trellis and to train plenty of climbing plants over it. If the fence belongs to a neighbour, the trellis might have to be supported on separate uprights. In addition to this, a small tree, specimen conifer or groups of mixed shrubs could be grown at intervals along the fence to increase screening where it is most needed and partly disguise the relatively long stretch of boundary.

An existing row of conifers

If a screen of well-established conifers already exists and is successfully hiding something, it might be too drastic an undertaking to remove them all and start again. There probably would not be sufficient time to re-grow an effective and more attractive screen before the next house move – very likely why the conifers were planted by the previous owners in the first place. A few conifers at either end of the row could, perhaps, be taken out and replaced with more attractive trees and some shrubs, or the front branches of one or more of the conifers could be cut hard back to make room for something more interesting in front, such as a variegated evergreen. The soil is, however, certain to be full of conifer roots and very dry so plants for this type of position will have to be selected very carefully.

Lighting

Introducing some artificial lighting into short, wide gardens is especially effective since the areas involved are so small and close to the house. Although white light is generally the most popular in gardens, some coloured lighting would be very effective in front of the planting along a rear boundary and also in a raised bed behind any seating.

Short and wide gardens on a slope

Any garden on a slope or on more than one level will tend to appear smaller than a flat one of equal size, so if your short, wide garden is on a slope the problem may seem even worse. If the garden is to be terraced it would be best to have as much on one level as is structurally possible. For a garden sloping down, away from the house, this would involve building a retaining wall very close to the rear fence and part way up each side then filling in with imported soil. For a garden sloping up and away from the house it could mean flattening the slope between two retaining walls. The first wall would be built about a path width out from the house and up to half the total height of the slope, together with some side retaining walls. The upper half of the slope would then be dug away from the rear boundary (providing this did not interfere with any neighbouring structures) and used to fill in against the first wall. A second retaining wall could then be built against the rear boundary and part of the

way along each side to hold back the neighbouring land. The result would be a garden on one elevated level which could then be set out along the lines already described.

Ideally, neither of these retaining walls should be higher than about 75cm (2ft 6in) in such a small area because the garden could seem too high and oppressive so close to the house. Gardens in which the overall height of the slope is more than about 1.5m (5ft) are better divided into two terraces with the largest being closest to the house and both being set at an angle rather than parallel to the boundaries.

It is often possible to restrict the size of potentially large plants by growing them on a patio in containers.

SHRUBS FOR GROWING UP AGAINST AN ESTABLISHED CONIFER SCREEN

The shrubs listed below, if planted in well-prepared soil and given plenty of water and feeding, will tolerate growing right up against an established conifer screen:

Aucuba japonica
Varieties with variegated leaves are very effective but all forms will grow large in time

Choisya ternata (Mexican orange blossom)
Clusters of white flowers in late spring. This will grow large in time

Cotoneaster lacteus
A large, evergreen species

Elaeagnus
Evergreen, with a choice of variagated or plain varieties

Euonymus japonicus and **E. fortunei**
Many varieties to choose from

Hedera (ivy)

Ilex (holly)

Kerria japonica 'Picta'
(Jew's mallow)

Euonymus fortunei

Ligustrum (privet)
Many types to choose from

Mahonia
All types are suitable

Pieris
Prefers a lime-free soil

Pleioblastus (bamboo)
These can grow quite large, particularly in width

Skimmia
Most types are suitable for this situation

Viburnum tinus
The form **'Variegatum'** has attractive, variegated leaves

Pieris formosa var. forrestii

Vinca major and **V. minor** (periwinkle)
Evergreen trailing shrub, good for ground cover, and will scramble up into nearby plants. A range of variegations and flower colours is available

Dealing with tiny sites

A tiny garden

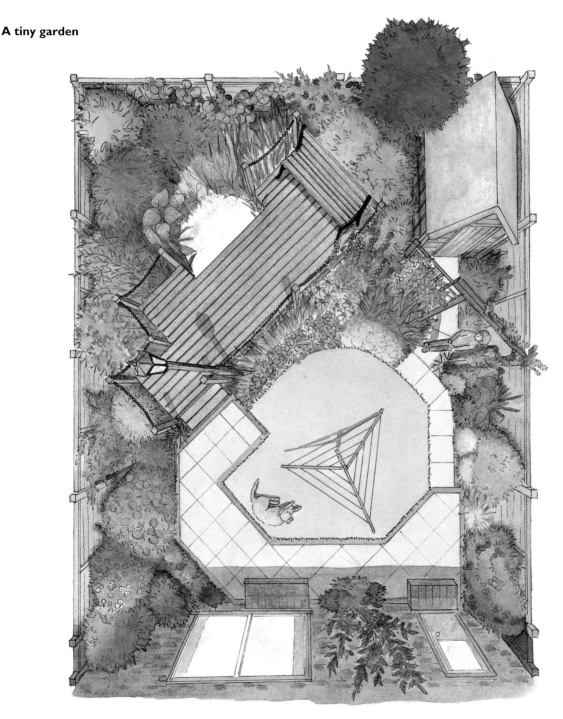

This garden lies behind a modern terraced house and has to accommodate a number of fixed and planting features as well as a dog.

A small back yard is one of the most rewarding types of garden to plan because you can treat it almost as another room of your house. It is often small enough to make a complete re-fit affordable and it is usually intimate enough for you to include a whole range of small, intricate features. A yard is usually surrounded by fences or a wall and is therefore sheltered enough for you to grow a wide range of plants, including some tender species. It will also be somewhere pleasant and sheltered for you to sit, even if it receives only a limited amount of sunshine.

Planning

Because there is so little space, you will have to measure your yard carefully and draw it to scale accurately on paper so that you can plan it just the way you want. It all depends on what you want to include. A sunlounger, for example, needs a space of at least 2.1m (7ft) long and 1m (3ft 3in) wide, so you would have to shape and position any patio paving accordingly. A rotary washing line must have a space with a diameter of at least 2.4 m (8ft) free from tall or prickly plants or any other obstructions. If you need a shed or greenhouse, with such little space, one of the 'cupboard' types that fit against a wall would be more appropriate than a conventional type. The two examples here are

of back yards which have been planned to accommodate a number of these features and several others besides, not to mention a good selection of plants.

A fenced back yard

The yard opposite is fenced rather than walled and is slightly less enclosed. If a garden like this belonged to a retired couple, they would want to fit in as many features as possible, so that there was always something interesting to look at. Once again, a diagonal lay-out has made it possible to include more than might have been possible with a 'straight-on' or rectangular one. The rotary washing line socket could hold a sunshade on occasions during the summer and the lawn, as before, could be used as a 'soft' patio.

Timber decking

This is relatively easy to construct, need not cost as much as some other types of paving and will make a very warm and comfortable patio surface. Timber decks are also very flexible when it comes to shaping – almost anything is possible which makes them especially suitable for a small garden. In some small gardens, a change of level can make the area seem even smaller, but in this example it has been successfully used to create an interesting feature.

Garden plan

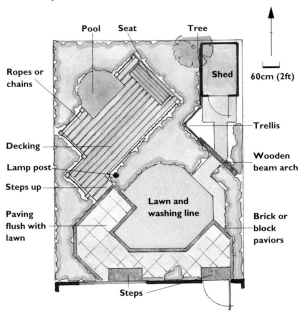

A diagonal lay-out has made it possible to fit a lot of garden features, including some lawn, in to a very small space. There are also plenty of opportunities for planting.

Much has been included in this small space, both in a lateral and vertical plane: there is room for garden furniture, flowers and planting of different heights.

These small paving setts are ideal for small-scale patio areas and can be used to create interesting patterns.

An area of decking has been elevated over some water so that the owner steps up on to it and will have a vantage point from which to view the rest of the garden. Unlike the moving water feature in the next yard (which creates a different aspect), this pond is still and tranquil. Unfortunately, being open, it is therefore unsafe for a garden in which small children play. It will, however, encourage pond life although in a completely walled garden, frogs and toads will have difficulty in reaching it from the outside world and will therefore have to be deliberately introduced.

Instead of the small shed, a greenhouse could have been included although the fence would keep it in the shade for some of the time. A 'cupboard' type greenhouse, bolted to a sunny wall, could help solve the problem, but in this garden the only available wall is in the shade. Unfortunately, in a yard, there is some shade all the time especially during the very beginning of the year when the sun is low in the sky.

Trellis and arches can be used to divide off small areas in a yard but they must never be too 'heavy' in their construction, otherwise they could look out of proportion to everything else.

Planting

This yard, like the next one shown, has a good selection of plants, although shade-tolerant ones would have to be used across the back of the house. The corner behind the pool could feature a collection of bog plants which, in time, would become a little overgrown and harbour wild life.

In general, the air in a yard can often be quite still even when it is relatively windy elsewhere so that, during the summer in particular, scented plants will seem even more fragrant than usual. Fragrance should therefore be given a high priority and you should include scented climbers, shrubs and herbs, or perhaps lilies growing in pots.

Walled yards, in particular, are likely to be warmer in winter (and summer) because the walls absorb heat from the sun during the day. Beds against the sunniest walls may rarely freeze, certainly not to any depth, making it possible to grow a number of plants that would probably not survive in the open garden, including *Agapanthus*, *Canna*, *Cordyline*, *Passiflora* (passion flower), *Callistemon* (bottle brush plant) and so on. On the other hand, clematis detest growing in borders exposed to the hot sun and would much prefer their roots, at least, in a cooler, shady place. Such a high concentration of plants would have to be fed during the growing season with a fertilizer containing trace elements as well as the usual nitrogen, phosphate and potash.

Now that timber can be pressure treated, decking can be used as a durable and permanent surface.

An alternative treatment of a tiny garden

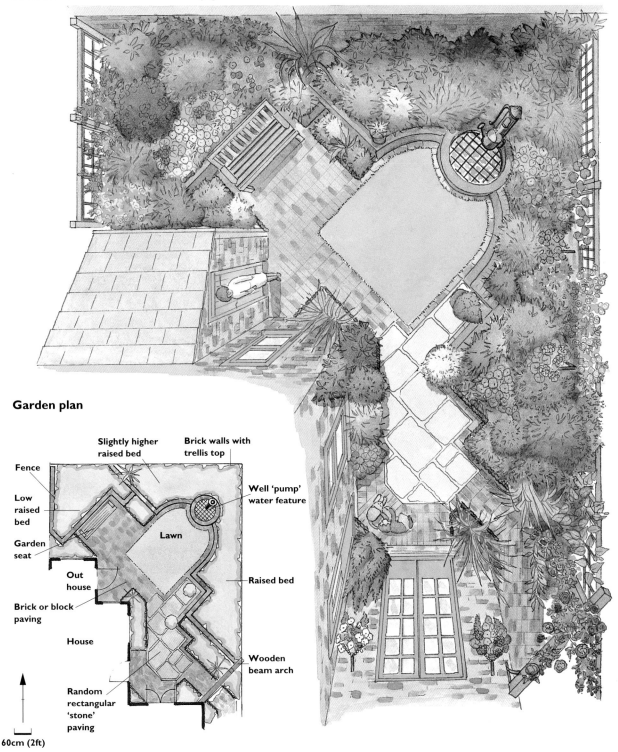

Garden plan

Slightly higher raised bed

Brick walls with trellis top

Fence

Well 'pump' water feature

Low raised bed

Lawn

Garden seat

Out house

Raised bed

Brick or block paving

House

Wooden beam arch

Random rectangular 'stone' paving

60cm (2ft)

As well as some interesting variations in height, this garden contains some lawn, paving, a child-safe water feature and some interesting planting.

This garden lies at the back of a small Victorian house. Despite the lack of space, the lay-out has provided plenty of room for sitting out and other garden activities. Although the lawn would not stand a great deal of wear and tear it does help to create a restful atmosphere.

A space-saving way to grow *Forsythia,* as well as many other shrubs and climbers, is to keep it trained against a trellis.

A walled back yard

The second yard illustrated is typical of the sort found at the rear of a Victorian semi-detached 'villa'. The out-house might once have been an outdoor toilet but can easily be converted into a garden store, which helps to save on space. The back of this house faces the mid-day sun so that, in summer, much of the yard would be sunny.

Lawns

It is always difficult to decide whether there is enough room for a lawn in such a small area. If there are children constantly playing in the yard then the answer would almost certainly be 'no', because wear and tear will rapidly reduce the grass to a sea of mud in wet weather. If it is not likely to be subjected to hard wear, then grass can help to cover the floor of the yard and reduce the amount of hard landscaping. In this lay-out there are no really extensive areas of paving, so the grass would double up as a patio for garden furniture on sunny days.

Walls and paving

Positioning the random rectangular stone paving at an angle along with most of the other features allows more to be fitted in to the area than would have been possible with a traditional rectangular lay-out. It does mean, however, that some slabs have to be cut and therefore edged with brick (or block paviors) for neatness. The variety of materials used in a small area should always be restricted so that the lay-out does not end up looking too complicated, disjointed and therefore even smaller than it really is. Apart from a small amount of timber, only brick and stone have been used here, producing a reasonably uncluttered result despite the various garden features.

Any garden wall which does not form part of a dwelling can be used as the rear wall of a raised bed. In this yard, raised beds extend around at least half of the garden. The one on the left-hand side is against a fence and would therefore need its own rear wall. The 'well' feature has a deep reservoir from which an electric submersible pump circulates water through the old iron pump and back again. The reservoir has been fitted with a heavy iron grill for safety.

The height of the wall on the right has been effectively increased by adding some trellis, although this is not always without problems. If the wall belongs to neighbours, they ought to be consulted first, and if the wall is in a very windy area and is not very strong, it is just possible that, once the trellis is covered with plants, it, together with the fixing stays, could pull the

Raised beds in a tiny garden can be planted with all manner of small and compact seasonal flowers and bulbs.

top half of the wall over in a strong wind. The risk of this can be reduced by running these stays, to which the trellis is fixed, right down to the bottom of the wall and, if they are metal, right into the ground.

The plants

All sorts of plants are growing in this yard including climbers, shrubs, ground-cover and trailing plants, bulbs, herbs, herbaceous plants and seasonal flowers in pots and hanging baskets.

Drainage

One problem with walled yards, especially in heavy clay, is the likelihood of poor drainage. It is quite possible that a lot of the roof water already goes into a soakaway within the yard, thus exhausting the ground's capacity to soak up any more. Paving surrounded by raised beds will have to be given some form of surface drainage, otherwise it could flood. In this example, water should be able to drain away through the few beds which are at paving level and, to some extent, through the lawn.

Every opportunity should be taken to use hanging baskets which will introduce colour and perhaps some vegetables to the smallest spaces.

Here, some *Convolvulus cneorum* and irises make an attractive combination without taking up a lot of space.

PLANTS FOR TUBS

Plants in tubs and containers are invaluable for back yards or gardens where space is at a premium. As most of a small garden is visible from the house, it is important to provide interest throughout the year. Here is a selection of suitable plants:

***Berberis x stenophylla* 'Corallina Compacta'**
Dwarf evergreen shrub with neat oval leaves. Tiny, bright orange flowers in late spring

***Chamaecyparis lawsoniana* 'Minima Glauca'**
Sea-green foliage. Height 35cm (14in)

Convolvulus cneorum
Evergreen with silky, silver-green leaves. White, yellow-centred flowers in the spring

Euonymus
Any of the evergreen varieties are ideal for tubs. Many have variegated foliage

Hebe
Evergreen shrubs with dense spikes of flowers. All varieties suitable for tubs

Salvia officinalis leterina

***Lavandula angustifolia* 'Hidcote'**
Evergreen shrib with fragrant, deep purple flowers mid- to late summer and aromatic silver-grey leaves

Salvia (sage)
Many varieties have brightly coloured flowers and leaves

Vinca (periwinkle)
Evergreen trailing shrub with variety of leaf and flower colour to choose from

Yucca
Bold, sword-shaped leaves and panicles of white flowers in mid- to late summer.

***Yucca* (variegated form)**

Making the most of sloping sites

A garden sloping down towards the house

Walls have been used here to retain the slope, create a range of interesting features and form a patio.

Sloping gardens may have no areas suitable for a garden seat or, for that matter, anything else which requires reasonably level ground such as a greenhouse, shed or pool. It may also be very awkward to do any gardening on a very steep slope, so some form of level terrace or patio will provide a useful sitting area as well as somewhere to garden with ease. Creating a patio on a slope will invariably require a good deal of physical effort and involve some expense. In general, the most obvious place to create a level area would be immediately adjacent to a door at the back (or side) of the house, although if this area is in shade most of the time another area of level ground could also be created in a sunnier part of the garden.

Gardens sloping up from the house

Where the garden slopes up and away from the back of the house then, obviously, ground will have to be cut away in order to create a level area. Where your slope is very steep, cutting back even a short distance will quickly result in quite a high bank of soil. You may, therefore, have to limit the depth and distance of this excavation and create another, higher level just a little further back. The windows and doors across the back of the house will then be spared an outlook onto a high, oppressive wall and instead a gentle series of attractively varying heights will be seen; the main patio area can be on the next level up.

Once again, the further this higher terrace extends, the more extensive the excavation required. A square or rounded area of patio is always more useful than a narrow strip of paving, so in many cases it would be much better to dig out further at one end rather than excavating the same distance right across. Even on a steep slope this will produce a patio on which it will be possible to arrange chairs or garden furniture in a sociable cluster rather than in a straight line across the back of the house.

Garden plan

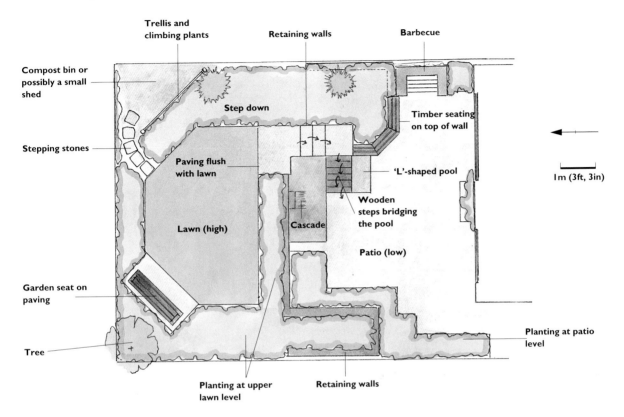

Trellis and climbing plants

Retaining walls

Barbecue

Compost bin or possibly a small shed

Step down

Timber seating on top of wall

Stepping stones

Paving flush with lawn

'L'-shaped pool

Lawn (high)

Cascade

Wooden steps bridging the pool

Patio (low)

Garden seat on paving

Tree

Planting at patio level

Planting at upper lawn level

Retaining walls

1m (3ft, 3in)

Retaining a garden using strong walls can be quite expensive but the space they create will provide the opportunity to accommodate features which would otherwise be difficult to build on a slope.

The excavated soil

Any excavation will produce a lot of soil. Some of this could well be useless subsoil, stones or rock while the rest might be good quality topsoil. Unless you are building more terraces further up the slope, the sub-soil can be taken away and any topsoil saved for patio beds or spread throughout the rest of the garden.

Cut and fill

Where the garden slopes less steeply, the patio will not go as far underground so the excavation will not yield so much spoil. Much of the excavated soil could there-fore be built up along the far edge of the new terrace, helping to level the next section of garden, although this will mean an increase in the height of any retain-ing wall and perhaps introduce the need for steps up. This technique is known as 'cut and fill' and can be useful whichever way the garden slopes. If possible, the topsoil from the built up part of this second

terrace area should be stripped back to reveal the sub-soil. The subsoil from the main excavation can then be put on top of this before any topsoil is replaced to produce good growing conditions. Straightforward though this procedure is in theory, excavation can unearth all sorts of problems including old founda-tions, pipes, cables even springs of running water.

Drainage

Drainage can be a major problem for patios which end up below ground level. Whereas rain might have drained away through the garden soil, paving is not porous so, with the help of a 'fall' away from the house, water is bound to collect along the lower edge against the bank or retaining walls. A system of drains will be essential in all except the sandiest of soils, linked to an efficient outfall which is capable of taking the water away quickly, even in a storm.

Gardens which slope down from the house

Gardens which slope down and away from the back of

A garden sloping down, away from the house

Here, two levels have helped to produce an attractive and relatively leisurely route down to the rest of the garden.

a house present a different set of problems. In order to create a level area next to the house, the ground will have to be built up. One problem with patios over made-up ground is that they can eventually subside and crack, so any filling must be based on top of firm ground and be of a material which can be compacted and not deteriorate. It is therefore important to remove any soft topsoil, then use well-compacted hardcore, rock or scalpings as a filling behind a suitably strong retaining wall.

Once the area nearest to the house has been built up, the view to the rest of the garden might have been obscured so it is a good idea to create, within the patio, beds of soil, perhaps raised, to accommodate a selection of plants. This will mean keeping some areas clear of hardcore so that they can be very easily filled with top soil. Steps will be needed down to the rest of the garden but drainage will not be a problem, since excess water can drain off the front edge of the patio, provided a suitable 'fall' is incorporated into the design.

Shaping is, once again, important, with construction concentrated into producing a useful area rather than a narrow, level strip right across the slope. A lack of privacy might be a problem on built-up patios since it could become possible to see over the top of any side fences and down into the neighbours' gardens on either side. Some extra trellis and climbing plants along the top of the existing fences would help here.

Walls

Although it is possible to retain (or protect) both types of patio with banks rather than walls, these can occupy too much valuable space in a small garden. Banks also may not be stable enough to prevent soil erosion or subsidence. Walls, though expensive, do make the best use of space and can be made highly decorative with the addition of built-in features such as railings, alcoves or even cascading water. Gardens on either side of the terraced area will have to be protected from all the changes of level. Where a patio has been cut into a slope, walls will be needed, not just to hold back the garden soil but also to prevent the soil (and fences) from neighbouring gardens from falling in on either side. A built-up patio will need retaining walls on either side, as well as along its front edge, to

Garden plan

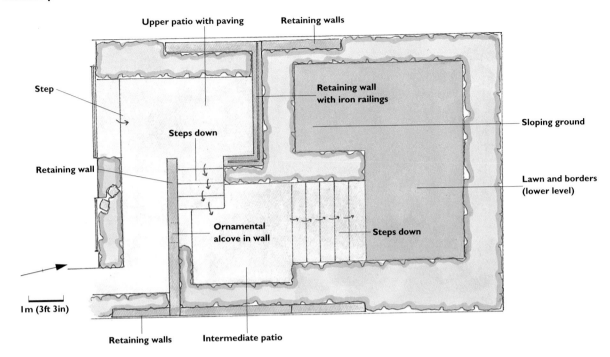

Upper patio with paving

Retaining walls

Step

Retaining wall with iron railings

Steps down

Sloping ground

Retaining wall

Lawn and borders (lower level)

Ornamental alcove in wall

Steps down

1m (3ft 3in)

Retaining walls   **Intermediate patio**

Splitting the drop into two terraces has helped to limit the height of individual walls and create two distinct patios.

prevent the weight of the soil used for infilling making the neighbours' fences collapse.

All walls must have good concrete foundations set well down in to firm ground. These walls should be at least 21.5cm (8½in) thick, perhaps with steel reinforcing rods coming up out of the foundation and set well up into a central cavity. Walls which are likely to block the natural passage of ground water or springs must be provided with weepholes through which this water can pass. It will be helpful to include some form of drainage material at the back to prevent these holes from becoming blocked.

Steps

Patios which are raised up on top of a slope, and in some cases cut into a slope, will need railings or some planting to prevent people, especially children, from falling over the edge, and all will need steps (again, possibly with railings or a handrail). Sometimes, particularly in the case of sunken patios, wooden steps or open stairs could be used, although if these extend higher than about 60cm (2ft) they should have a handrail for extra safety.

In general, steps can travel in one (or both) of two directions – from front to back, straight out in to the garden, or sideways across the garden, left to right. On large patios, both styles might be possible. It is important to remember that every time a step rises by, say, 15cm (6in) it will have to travel forward by at least 30cm (12in). A flight of steps could therefore travel a long way forward and, in a small garden (or patio), might use up too much valuable space. The alternative is to run the steps up sideways, across the face of the wall, with some space both at the top and bottom for a 'landing'.

Patio features

It is often more practical to build one large patio which can accommodate a number of garden features than to create several smaller plateaux around the garden to fulfil different functions. Apart from a sitting and dining area and some space for planting flowers or greenery, a single large patio could accommodate a shed, a greenhouse, a barbecue, a water feature, a sand-pit and children's play area, and anything else which needs a reasonably level base.

Materials

Any of those materials normally associated with patio construction can be used for patios on a slope, although large areas of shingle might be trodden indoors or be kicked off over the edge of a raised patio. All parts of the walls which can be seen will, of course, have to be built from attractive materials but less expensive materials, such as concrete blocks, can be used in areas which are out of sight.

Planting

For raised patios, fairly tall wall shrubs and climbers trained up trellis on either side can help to increase privacy, whereas planting to the side of a sunken patio

These steps provide an attractive way of joining two levels within a circular lay-out although, without a handrail, they would be unsuitable for young children or the elderly. Stepping back the terraces lets in more light than having one high wall.

should be chosen to soften the effect of what will appear to be quite high fences or boundary walls. All patios on a slope have the potential to accommodate a number of trailing plants, so space should be created along all the appropriate edges. If the patio is against a house, the house walls are likely to be a dominant feature and would benefit from climbing plants, together with some lower planting at ground level.

On hot sunny patios, some of these climbers can be encouraged to grow onto a pergola to provide some leafy, dappled shade. There are various small trees (and conifers) suitable for a patio planting, including *Acer japonicum* (Japanese maple) and small magnolias. Both require a sheltered position and deep, fertile soil. Various small weeping trees would be ideal used together with a selection of ground-cover plants, or collections of bonsai trees, perhaps, in association with alpines. Damp, sunken patios are ideal for some

of the smaller hostas, primulas and a collection of ferns. Whatever the style of patio, there should always be room for bedding plants to provide an attractive display for a large part of the year.

Raised patios in particular can become very dry and they certainly benefit from some form of automatic watering. There are various mini-computerized systems which can simply be supplied by an outside tap and linked to trickle nozzles and 'spaghetti' lines. The unit can then be programmed to water (and feed) all the beds, pots, tubs and even hanging baskets for as often and as long as necessary. This is particularly useful if you go away on holiday.

These steps are coming down into a shady, damp area. It would therefore be important to use paving with a relatively non-slip surface under these circumstances. Plants like this *Hosta crispula* will thrive here.

Another sloping garden

A variety of materials, including wooden railway sleepers, have been used for terracing here.

PLANTS FOR RETAINING WALLS

Here are some plants that will grow over and hang down the face of a retaining wall:

Arabis
Mainly pink or white flowers in spring, semi-evergreen green or variegated foliage. Height 15cm (6in)

Aubrieta
Pink, red, purple or white flowers in spring. Height 15cm (6in)

Ceanothus x thyrsiflorus repens
Spreading mats of evergreen foliage with blue flowers in late spring. Height 25cm (10in)

Aubrieta – mixed colours

Cotoneaster dammeri var. radicans
Mats of glossy, evergreen foliage and red berries. Height 25cm (10in)

Euonymus fortunei 'Emerald Gaiety'
Spreading evergreen foliage, variegated white and green. Height 30cm (1ft)

Genista pilosa
Forms a semi-evergreen mat of grey-green foliage covered in yellow flowers in early summer. Height 25cm (10in)

Euonymus fortunei

Lithodoro 'Heavenly Blue'
Mat of dark evergreen foliage and small, intensely blue flowers in summer. Requires acid soil. Height 15cm (6in)

Don't stick solely to these plants. Numerous prostrate conifers, particularly junipers, and alpines, as well as thymes can be considered when planning a retaining wall.

Coping with shade

Shade at the back of a house

Garden plan

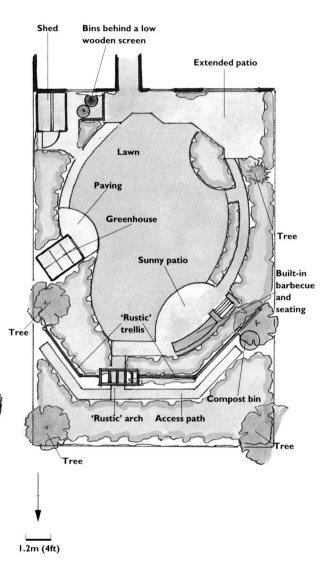

Careful planning can ensure that features like a greenhouse and a patio, along with sun-loving plants, are given the sunniest positions in a garden.

The main patio next to the house has been extended to reach beyond the shaded area and a further patio/barbecue area positioned to catch the sun later in the day.

Both the sundial and the seat have been carefully positioned so that they are away from the shade.

All gardens have some areas of shade, but small gardens often have more than most because of the proximity of neighbouring walls and fences. However, although shade can reduce the performance of some plants and restrict certain recreational activities, it need not necessarily hinder the development of a beautiful and interesting garden. There are plenty of plants that actually relish shade

Assessing shade

Make a note of where the shadows fall in your garden at various times of the day, and different times of year, particularly during spring and summer. In winter, shadows are longer and larger areas will therefore be without sun, but for the majority of plants which become dormant in winter, this will not matter. During the spring and summer, however, plants will be growing actively and need a certain amount of sunlight. You are also likely to be spending a lot more

time outdoors at this time of the year and may well want to relax in the sun, so finding out which parts of the garden receive sun at various times of the day will be of particular interest from spring onwards. You will find that some areas of your garden are always in shade, some are partially shaded and others in full sun. It is in the permanently shaded areas that you will have to take most care with your choice of plants.

Designing around shade

Shade is usually regarded in a rather negative way but, if your design and planting are planned to take account of the varying light levels, you will find that areas of shade are just as rewarding in the garden as the sunnier parts. The important thing is to make the best use of what light you do have.

Sometimes an island bed can be the best way of accommodating plants away from areas of deep shade.

ACID-LOVING SHRUBS FOR TREE CANOPIES

Many acid-loving plants (known as ericaceous) such as rhododendrons, azaleas, pieris, camellias and others grow and flower well beneath some of the less dense trees, provided that the soil has a pH value of less than about 6.5. Apart from testing the soil with an appropriate kit or meter, one way of researching which plants grow best beneath trees in your area is to walk around and see what has succeeded in other people's gardens or the park. This will not only help you to make the best choice, but will also help you to avoid expensive mistakes.

Rhododendron
All types can be grown provided they receive some light and moisture

Camellia
These also prefer some light and moisture

Camellia williamsii

Gaultheria
This is a good choice of evergreen ground cover

Pieris
All types will grow but they prefer moisture

Vaccinium vitis-idaea
This is good for ground cover

Pieris 'Flaming Silver'

Some people will choose to devote the sunniest places of their garden to a patio or seat. For those who work during the day, a patch of evening sunshine could be more important than one in mid-day sun. For plant-lovers, a greenhouse, cold-frame, fruit, vegetables and certain flower crops will take up the sunniest places. A greenhouse which is to be used for raising seedlings will need sun or good light in very early spring. If, on the other hand, the greenhouse is only used to overwinter plants or for a few tomatoes during the summer, it need not receive any significant sun until late spring and, even then, only for part of the day, preferably the morning. A vegetable patch which is not brought into serious cultivation until late spring could be more in the shade than, say, a cold frame which is used for very early lettuce.

There are times when shade is a positive advantage. Shrubs which flower in winter or early spring, such as camellias and peaches, may lose their flowers in frosty weather if the sun catches them early in the morning and thaws them out too quickly, so these plants should not be planted on a wall that faces the early morning sun. Don't forget that there are plenty of plants that will positively thrive in shady places but if you don't want to take advantage of these many shade-lovers, you can always have a path, shed or compost heap in a shady area.

Different types of shade
It is important to recognize that there are different types of shade and to select appropriate plants for the different sites. Perhaps the most restricting situation for plant growth is beneath tree canopies, not so much because of the lack of light but because of the lack of moisture. *Aesculus hippocastanum* (horse chestnut), *Castanea sativa* (sweet chestnut), *Fagus sylvatica* (beech), *Quercus robur* (oak) and large conifers like *Cedrus* spp. (cedars) are among the worst, being dense and thirsty growers. If you have any of these larger trees in your garden, with several well-established but perhaps uninteresting shrubs growing underneath, think twice before taking them out and planting something new, for it is quite likely that the shrubs were planted when the trees were much smaller and the situation less inhospitable, so to replace them would be difficult. It could take a long time for new plants (even shade-tolerant ones) to become established. *Betula pendula* (birch) and *Sorbus aucuparia* (mountain ash) cast much less dense shade and therefore are less of a problem. For any type of

Dappled shade for some of the day may suit certain plants better than deep shade or bright sunshine.

planting under trees, thorough ground preparation and watering during the summer will help.

The shade cast by a garden fence or wall is usually far less extensive than that cast by trees, although it will still limit the performance of some plants. The shady side of a hedge has the added problem of dry soil and roots, coupled with the fact that, at certain times of the year, before it is trimmed back, it will be wider. Very often, when a garden is redesigned around an existing established hedge, it is worth leaving a 45–60cm (18–24in) unplanted strip running along the length of the hedge as an access path to allow maintenance to be carried out. This also means that plants will not be introduced too closely to the hedge.

Shade from a house is usually much more extensive as well as being dense, and there are often nooks and crannies which never seem to receive any sun at all. Apart from the restrictions this places on plants, it can also cause problems with paving. Both natural stone and timber decking in dense shade often stay wet after rain, may become slippery with algae and, in winter, the persistent moisture can turn to ice. Paving in the shade should, ideally, have a relatively non-slip surface, so bricks, block paviors and rough-textured surfaces should help.

Shady lawns

Shade from a building or boundary does not seem to suppress the growth of grass and, in hot summer weather, this type of shade may actually protect the lawn from being scorched, even when the ground is

HERBACEOUS PLANTS FOR THE EDGE OF TREE CANOPIES

Bergenia cordifolia

Brunnera macrophylla

Convallaria majalis (lily-of-the-valley)

Digitalis purpurea (foxglove)

Epimedium Add plenty of acid humus to the soil

Geranium (cranesbill) Most types will grow in lightly shaded areas

Digitalis purpurea

Helleborus (Christmas or Lenten rose) The soil must not be too dry

Iris foetidissima (Gladwin or stinking iris) This is grown mainly for its seed pods with bright orange, fleshy seeds

Lamium galeobdolon (dead nettle) There are many variations of this which are also appropriate. Make sure the soil is humus-rich

Liriope muscari (lilyturf)

Omphalodes verna

Ophiopogon planiscapus 'Nigrescens' (black grass) This black, grass-like plant likes humus

Helleborus

Symphytum ibericum (comfrey)

Tricyrtis formosana (toad lily) Some ferns will tolerate dry conditions, and most of the prostrate junipers do well at the edge of a tree canopy

Where shade results from overhanging trees, the soil may become rather dry and therefore restrict plant choice.

very dry. Shade from overhanging trees, however, will often suppress the growth of grass and encourage moss. But it is possible to cultivate a good lawn even in shady conditions with some scarifying (removing any thatch of grass by vigorously raking with a spring-tined rake so that air can enter the soil surface) and a couple of high nitrogen feeds applied before the tree's leaves open out and prevent rain from reaching the ground and washing any more fertilizer in. The lawn will, however, often run out of food and water by mid-summer unless irrigated.

The use of a shade mixture of grasses should also be considered for areas under large trees, although the resulting lawn may still be rather sparse and disappointing. Shade grasses should only be cut occasionally and are best left to grow into a semi-wild area with some naturalized wild flowers and bulbs. For areas of lawn in shade that are to be mown regularly, it is often better to persist with an ordinary lawn grass mixture, feeding, watering and scarifying whenever necessary.

Although certain plants and grass can be grown in deep shade, sometimes it is more practical to use paving instead of grass.

CLIMBING ROSES FOR SHADY WALLS

Certain varieties are suitable for growing against shady walls, including **'Danse du Feu'** (orange red), **'Etoile de Hollande Climbing'** (deep red), **'Gloire de Dijon'** (yellow), **'Golden Showers'** (yellow), **'Guinée'** (deep scarlet), **'Madame Alfred Carrière'** (white), **'Madame Grégoire Staechelin'** (pink) and **'Maigold'** (deep yellow)

'Madame Alfred Carrière'

PLANTS FOR SHADY MOIST SITES

Where the shade is moist (that is to say, away from trees) grow any of the following:

***Aralia elata* 'Variegata'** (variegated Japanese angelica tree)
This needs plenty of headroom, about 2.7m (9ft)

***Aucuba japonica* 'Variegata'** (spotted laurel)
If allowed, this will grow up to 2.5m (8ft)

***Corylus maxima* 'Purpurea'** (purple-leafed hazel)

Elaeagnus
All types grow quite large, up to 3–5m (10–16ft)

Pachysandra terminalis
This, and the variegated form, are all suitable if grown in humus-rich soil

***Photinia x fraseri* 'Red Robin'**
This grows best in moist soil

Pleioblastus (bamboo)
This may be slow to grow but is well worth the wait

Prunus lusitanica (Portugal laurel)
The variegated form will also grow well in these conditions

Ribes sanguineum (flowering currant)
Avoid this in very dry places

Rubus cockburnianus (ornamental blackberry or bramble)
This has very attractive white stems in winter

Sambucus nigra (common elder)

Euphorbias, ornamental grasses , shade-tolerant shrubs and woody ground-cover plants (such as box) can also be grown.

It is important to distinguish between dry and moist shade and select the plants accordingly. The plants shown here would prefer moist soil.

Planting in the shade

Plants are seldom actually killed by dense shade but those that require brighter conditions may certainly not give of their best. If you know which plants are suited to various garden conditions, however, you should be able to design plantings for every part of your garden, including the shaded areas.

Generally speaking, the aspect of plant growth most likely to be adversely affected by too much shade is flowering. A wisteria, for example, will grow vigorously in a sunless position but it will not flower anywhere near as freely as it would if it were growing in the sun. Mahonia, on the other hand, can flower profusely, even in deep shade. Plant growth is also sometimes affected by shade, especially beneath trees. Most members of the dianthus family (pinks and carnations) dislike deep shade and produce leggy, straggly stems. Intensity of foliage colour may, in many cases, be more subdued in shade. *Spiraea japonica* 'Gold Flame' is bright gold in the sun but a dull yellow in shade. On the other hand, *Sambucus nigra* 'Marginata' (variegated elder) retains brilliant variegation, even beneath quite dark trees, although its vigour will be significantly reduced.

PLANTS FOR THE EDGE OF SHADED AREAS

Choisya ternata (Mexican orange blossom)

Cotoneaster dammeri var. radicans
This is good for ground cover

Hebe pinguifolia 'Pagei'
This is a particularly attractive hebe with grey leaves

Rubus tricolor (blackberry or bramble)
This is useful ground cover

Sarcococca humilis (Christmas or sweet box)

Spiraea japonica 'Anthony Waterer'

Symphoricarpos
All types grow well at the edge of a shady area

PLANTS FOR GROWING AGAINST SHADY WALLS

Certain plants will grow happily against a shady wall.

Chaenomeles speciosa (flowering quince)

Clematis
These prefer to have their roots in shade and their tops in sun

Cotoneaster horizontalis (fishbone cotoneaster)
Its variegated form is also suitable

Hedera (ivy)
Ivy is self-clinging and may damage old walls or fences

Hydrangea petiolaris (climbing hydrangea)
This is also self-clinging

Jasminum nudiflorum (winter-flowering jasmine)

Jasminum officinale (summer jasmine)
This is moderately successful provided the shade is not too dense

Hedera helix

Parthenocissus henryana (Virginia creeper)
This is self-clinging

DROUGHT-RESISTANT PLANTS FOR SHADY AREAS

Buxus sempervirens
This and its variegated forms are appropriate and grow well on chalk

Leycesteria formosa (Himalayan honeysuckle)
This prefers humus and some light

Lonicera nitida (hedge honeysuckle)
The golden form can also be grown, although 'Baggensen's Gold' may go green

Ruscus aculeatus (butcher's broom)
This is a curious, low-growing evergreen

Vinca (periwinkle)
All types are extremely useful as ground cover

Creating woodland

A garden among trees

A seat, paths and shade-tolerant shrubs have been used to create a secluded woodland area at one end of a town garden.

To find mature trees in a town garden is a real bonus for anyone looking for their own piece of countryside in an urban setting but developing a woodland garden can take a good deal of skill and hard work.

Tree preservation orders

There are many districts, mainly in and around towns, where any large trees which can be seen and appreciated by the people living nearby are protected by law - usually by a tree preservation order (TPO) or by the fact that they are growing within a conservation area. This usually means that, if you own these trees, you must seek permission from the district council to cut off any branches or carry out any other form of tree surgery. The law protects the whole tree and the ground (and roots) beneath the canopy of branches. It forbids any permanent construction, changes in

ground level, deep cultivation, the storage of heavy materials, bonfires or anything else which might harm the tree. There are heavy fines for anyone caught contravening these rules, but the law would not necessarily hinder the development of a simple woodland garden.

Clearing undergrowth

Only certain plants can thrive beneath large trees and even these may take many years to grow and develop. If you find dense undergrowth and scrub beneath large trees, you may be tempted to clear it all out, but a much more cautious approach would be better. You could certainly dig out or try to kill brambles, nettles and other common weeds but any shrubs including *Sambucus* (elder), *Corylus* (hazel), *Taxus* (yew) and *Buxus* (box) should be left for the time being in case you

Garden plan

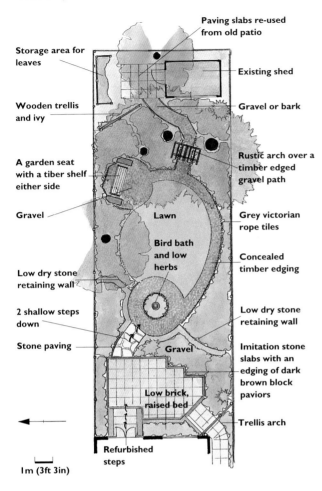

Storage area for leaves

Wooden trellis and ivy

A garden seat with a tiber shelf either side

Gravel

Low dry stone retaining wall

2 shallow steps down

Stone paving

Paving slabs re-used from old patio

Existing shed

Gravel or bark

Rustic arch over a timber edged gravel path

Grey victorian rope tiles

Lawn

Bird bath and low herbs

Concealed timber edging

Low dry stone retaining wall

Imitation stone slabs with an edging of dark brown block paviors

Low brick, raised bed

Gravel

Trellis arch

Refurbished steps

1m (3ft 3in)

This shows how a sunny flower garden can gradually be changed to become a woodland area.

need them, in the short term, while your new planting is becoming established. Before you draw up any planting plans you should ascertain whether your soil is acid or alkaline, by carrying out a pH test, the kit or meter for which you can buy at your local garden centre. New plants will have enough of a struggle to establish themselves without the added complication of being planted in the wrong soil. You may have to accommodate a shed and a compost bin or heap in your town woodland garden, but if these are to be positioned within the area of trees, they must be out of the way and placed where they cannot damage tree roots.

Paths

As with any type of garden, you will want to be able to walk through and enjoy your woodland area, so a

path or route winding its way between selected trees, perhaps ending at the shed or going around and coming back to where it started could be the next phase of your project. An earth path merely raked clear of debris would do, but you will find a timber or log-edged, 60cm (2ft) wide path of bark chippings or shingle can look very attractive and will be easier to walk on in wet weather. The bark chips or shingle could be placed directly on top of compacted soil but if the soil is sandy, it would be best to rake some cement dust into the top few centimetres (inch or two) before you compact it. This will produce a more stable base than plain soil alone.

Woodland features

In larger areas of 'woodland' you can develop a small grassy glade using a shade mixture of grass seed and incorporate a seat and naturalize some bulbs, such as narcissi and bluebells. If the entrance to the wooded area is poorly defined, except for the presence of a path, you could introduce a 'rustic' arch or small pergola as an entrance feature. A 'rustic' construction using pressure-treated poles and a planting of clematis and honeysuckle would fit into the woodland scene.

Woodland paths can be created from bark chips and edged with logs. Although oak or ash logs would last longer than the birch shown here the birch is very decorative.

Log stepping stones can be used as an attractive and informal woodland path but may become slippery or, like log edging, introduce honey fungus into the garden.

If there is an existing, shallow ditch running through the area, you could construct a small bridge over it, and there are a number of native ferns and wild flowers (depending on where your garden is situated) which you could introduce to turn it into an attractive and interesting feature. If there is no ditch, you might be able to create one without infringing a preservation order, but do check with the relevant planning authority before starting work.

If your woodland area does not have any old, gnarled tree stumps, you could introduce some from elsewhere to accommodate more ferns and mosses, and to add a sculptural dimension to the garden. Imported stumps may, however, also bring in an infection of *Armillaria mellea*, or honey fungus, which might then spread and damage some of the trees and shrubs.

Honey fungus (*Armillaria mellea*)

This is one of the most common fungal diseases of trees and shrubs in many parts of Europe, particularly in the cooler, moist zones. It lives in the soil and feeds, for most of the time, on decaying wood. From time to time, however, it will switch to feeding on the roots of living plants, eventually killing them in the process. A typical symptom would be for a whole branch or section of a tree or shrub to suddenly die off during the summer, with the leaves brown and withered but still attached. *Ligustrum* (privet) hedges sometimes display very clear symptoms with, initially, a small section going brown and the plants immediately either side turning yellow. Eventually, the plants in both directions will die and turn brown, but the infection may take several years to travel only a short distance and not affect anything else.

The fungus does have fruiting bodies (and therefore spores), and these can be seen as clusters of small, rounded honey-coloured mushrooms at or just above ground level on dead or decaying wood, mostly in the late summer and autumn. If you peel back the dead bark close to ground level, black, flattened 'branches' of the fungus might be visible underneath. There is not much you can do to eliminate the fungus but you can avoid bringing it into the garden in the first place by not bringing in rotten wood which could be affected – a risk with old stumps and logs. If you do choose to bring in old wood, check it carefully first.

An opposite view up the same garden

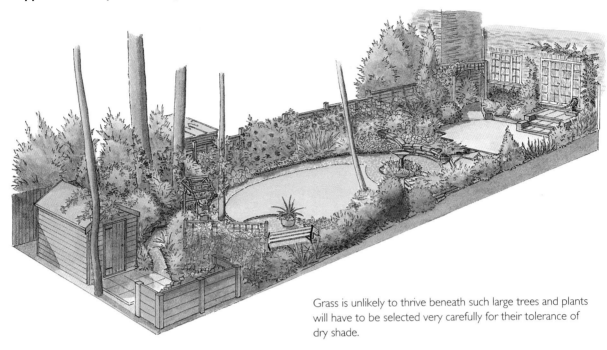

Grass is unlikely to thrive beneath such large trees and plants will have to be selected very carefully for their tolerance of dry shade.

A Garden lay-out

The presence of trees in a garden will obviously affect the rest of your lay-out. You patio area will have to be well away from the trees, partly because construction might damage the roots, but mainly, of course, because the trees will cast unwanted shadows. There are many plants that cannot thrive beneath trees, particularly the majority of herbaceous plants, herbs, roses, alpines, annuals and many shrubs so you will have to provide adequate border space for these away from the trees. Ponds and rock gardens should also be kept well away from the trees but you can, with some effort and using a special shade grass-seed mixture, cultivate a lawn under even quite dense tree canopies although it may turn brown during the height of summer.

In the garden illustrated above, the bottom third of the garden has been devoted to woodland-type planting. The patio is in full sun, but a bench seat has been positioned further down the garden under a tree, which will provide some shade. The garden is on a gentle slope down to the trees but any levelling or terracing has been restricted to the area nearest the house so that tree roots are not affected by construction or changes in level. Planting in the borders by the house and to about halfway down the garden is very mixed and colourful, but gives way to plants which will tolerate dry, shady conditions nearer the trees.

This picket fence would blend unobtrusively within a woodland garden but should be kept its natural wood colour and not painted white.

Shade

Trees do, of course, vary in their density of foliage and this will influence the performance of any plant growing underneath. A low, dense canopy of branches will be far more restricting than a high, light canopy. An established *Aesculus* (horse chestnut) will therefore restrict your choice of underplanting more than, say, a *Sorbus* (mountain ash) or a *Betula* (birch). If you remove the lowest branches of large, dense trees (with permission if necessary) you will let in more light and help to improve growing conditions although the ground underneath large trees will still be very dry.

Planting

The lack of light and moisture means that you will have to select your plants very carefully, and you must also take account of the soil pH value. If the soil is acid, then you may be able to grow a whole range of ericaceous plants successfully, including rhododendrons, azaleas and camellias. If, on the other hand, the soil is alkaline, the choice and range of plants will be more limited.

If your woodland garden is in a town, you may have fences to cover and a shed or compost area to screen. The list of plants which will grow beneath trees includes climbers, tall, medium and low shrubs, ground-cover plants and quite a few herbaceous plants. Some will be more tolerant of the conditions than others, so you will have to plant the least tolerant towards the edge of the tree canopy where there is more light and moisture.

Before you dig out any of the existing 'wild' shrubs, make a note of what they are and how successfully they are growing, as this could give you a clue as to which shrubs will grow well there. If, for example, *Sambucus* (elder) is growing well in its 'wild' form, then the variegated and purple-leafed forms should thrive successfully as well. If a plain green *Taxus* (yew) is thriving, then so should the golden form, and so on.

Preparing the ground

Dig out or kill off any invasive perennial weeds (if you haven't done so already), and cut back or remove any existing shrubs which are not needed for screening or as a framework for your new planting. Wherever possible, and without damaging too many tree roots, dig the ground over and add plenty of well-rotted manure, as this will help to store valuable moisture during any dry spells.

There are several ferns and various ground-cover plants which will thrive beneath or at the edge of an area of shrubs in a woodland garden.

Aftercare

All the new garden plants, whether or not they are beneath the trees, will benefit from summer watering and feeding. If you have done your planting at the best time – in the autumn – then growth should start early in the spring. Spring-planted shrubs may be much slower to grow away. It would be quite normal for growth on most shrubs to be relatively slow and limited during the first year or two, especially under trees, but after that, provided you feed and water in summer, the plants should grow normally and begin to fill out quite quickly.

Encouraging wildlife

The increased variety of plants should encourage more birds so you could consider putting up nesting boxes designed for various types of bird. Position a bird table in a more open part of the garden, preferably in a position where you can view it from the house, and put up a bat box on the house or high up on a large tree. Leave a haphazard pile of old mossy bricks in a corner somewhere to attract frogs and toads, and a pile of logs or a shed with a gap beneath the floor may provide a cosy bed for hibernating hedgehogs.

Where trees give way to more open conditions, it may be possible to develop a boggy area.

PLANTS TOLERANT OF DRY SHADE

Aucuba japonica (Japanese laurel)

Brachyglottis Dunedin hybrid – **'Sunshine'**

Buxus (box)

Cotoneaster frigidus 'Cornubia', *C. lacteus, C. × watereri*
All tree-type cotoneasters

Euonymus fortunei
E. japonicus

Gaultheria
Prefers an acid soil

Hamamelis (witch hazel)
Prefers an acid soil

Hedera (ivy)

Hypericum calycinum
(rose of Sharon)
May not flower in deep shade

Ilex (holly)

Kerria japonica 'Picta'

Lamium galeobdolon

Laurus nobilis (bay)

Leycesteria formosa
(pheasant berry)

Ligustrum ovalifolium (privet)

Lonicera nitida and ***L. pileata***

Mahonia
All types are suitable

Pachysandra terminalis
'Variegata'
Prefers an acid soil

Philadelphus (mock orange)
Not suitable for very dry sites

Photinia
All types are suitable

Pieris
Most types are suitable. Prefers an acid soil

Pleioblastus (bamboo)

Prunus laurocerasus (laurel)

Ribes odoratum and ***R.***
sanguineum (flowering currant)

Rhododendron
(including azaleas)
Prefers an acid soil. Very tolerant of shade but not always of dry conditions

Rubus (blackberry or bramble)

Sambucus (elder)
Not suitable for very dry conditions

Sarcococca (sweet box)
Prefers an acid soil

Skimmia
Most types are suitable

Euonymus japonicus

Kerria japonica 'Picta'

Philadelphus

Ribes sanguineum

Planning for parking

A front garden car park
The front garden of this north-facing house has had to be devoted almost entirely to car parking and access but, despite this, it has been possible to include some garden and to make it look attractive.

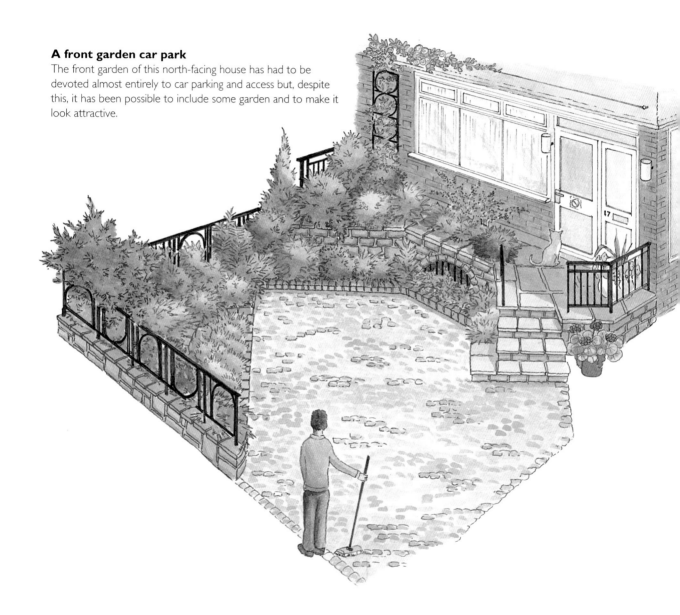

There are many front gardens (like the one featured above) which, first and foremost, have to accommodate a parked car while also leaving room for visitors and deliveries. In many cases, there may be so little room left over that you might imagine it would be impossible to make a garden. However, it is very often possible with the help of some careful planning and landscaping to have an appreciable amount of planting as well as space for a car and everything else. With careful shaping and a suitable choice of materials, even the parking area can be made to look like a garden rather than a car park when the car is not there.

Garden plan

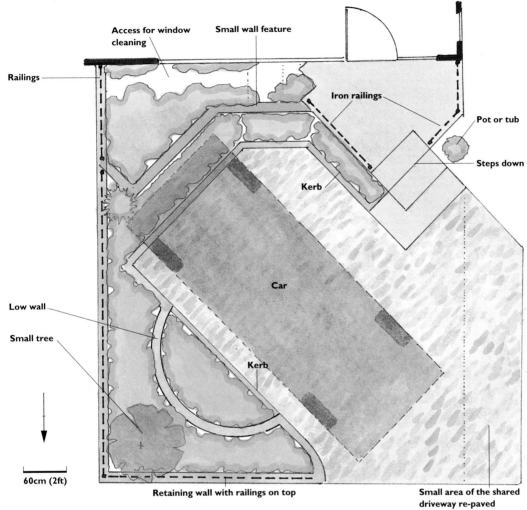

Access for window cleaning

Small wall feature

Railings

Iron railings

Pot or tub

Steps down

Kerb

Low wall

Small tree

Car

Kerb

60cm (2ft)

Retaining wall with railings on top

Small area of the shared driveway re-paved

The space needed to park a car and to use the front door has been very carefully analysed so as to avoid excessive areas of less attractive paving.

Working to scale

No space can be wasted, so you will need an accurate survey of the whole area and a plan that you can draw on paper to a scale of about 1cm:50cm (¼in:1ft). It should then be possible for you to plan to the nearest few centimetres (inches) and predict exactly where everything can go and how much space it will require. The overall dimensions of a car will also be needed along with the following information:

(i) how far back the front wheels are from the front bumper (assuming that the car will always be driven in forwards. If you back your car in, then it will be the distance between the rear wheels and the rear bumper)

(ii) how far back the front door hinges are from the

front wheels (or, again, rear door hinges from the rear wheels)

(iii) how much space you need at the side of the car to open the doors and get in and out

(iv) the height the bumpers are from the ground.

It might be prudent to use the dimensions of a large car, possibly larger than the one you normally park there so that a larger car could, if necessary, be parked comfortably at some time in the future.

Some other, more general measurements may be needed. For example:

(i) the size of a wheeled bin or dust bin (if you need one there)

(ii) how many steps, if any, you would need up to (or down to) the front door

(iii) the precise dimensions and positions of existing trees, hedges, meter cupboards, drains and any other permanent features.

You will also find it helpful to make a cardboard cut-out of the car to the same scale as the plan so that you can move it around on the plan when you are trying out different ideas.

Driving in off a road

Unless gates are to be fixed across the entrance, a wide entry off the road will be particularly useful – at least 2.4m (8ft) across and preferably more. This would make it possible to drive the car in at an angle and park it without too much manoeuvring, as opposed to driving in straight and parking at an angle, which is not easy in a small garden with more limited access. In most cases, parking at an angle is more useful than parking straight (at 90° to the house).

The other advantage of having a wide entrance is that you will not have to drive the car in any further than is required to ensure that the rear bumper is just

Any tall plants should be kept well away from the edges of a driveway.

clear of the pavement. With the extra width, there should still be room for visitors to walk past the rear corner of the car. In fact, if you have allowed enough space for a particularly large car, the bumper should end up comfortably inside the garden. The garden illustrated here has much the same situation but it took several attempts to find the angle which suited both the car and everything else.

Space for parking

Your parking bay need not, in theory, extend beyond the front wheels of a parked car although, in practice, it is better to err on the safe side and be just a little more generous with the paving than that. The plan of this garden shows a degree of flexibility in this respect but the front wheels are tight up against the edge of the parking bay. This means that it will be possible to have some planting space which is, for some of the time, partly beneath the front end of the car.

On one side of the car, the paving will extend right out and become the main route to and from the front door and other parts of the garden. In this garden, it happens to be on the right-hand side. If possible, there should be paving on the other side of the car (essential if this happens to be the driver's side), at least 60cm (2ft) wide so that people can get in and out. If this turns out to be the passenger's side, and if having as

The majority of plants around the driveway should be relatively low growing and, wherever possible, look attractive all the year round.

A small feature at the edge of the driveway

much garden as possible is a priority for you, then you could include slightly less paving on your plan than this and passengers would have to shuffle across to get in and out from the main access side. In addition, you do not need to have quite so much paving immediately alongside the bonnet so that, overall, the whole parking area can be tailored to leave you as much garden as possible. It will mean, however, that the car has to be parked with some precision despite a built-in degree of flexibility.

The paved surface

Although much of the paving will be underneath your car for some of the time there will also be areas, such as the main access to the front door, which will always be visible. It has often been the case in the past that the paving on which the car is parked is different from the rest but, in a garden lay-out like this one, the area will seem much larger if you use the same material all over, and the foundation underneath the paving could easily be made stronger to take the weight of a car. Standard, rectangular bevelled edge concrete block paviors are often used for driveways but these can be seen in a vast number of commercial, municipal and industrial car parks. There are other types of blocks and paving materials which are far more attractive and much more suited to a domestic situation but they would have to be given an appropriate foundation. In the example illustrated here, a 'rustic' cobble or sett, made from concrete but looking like stone, has been used with a chunky stone sett kerb.

This mock culvert has been incorporated to make the retaining wall more interesting and to help to make as much as possible of what little garden there is.

Dwarf conifers are particularly useful plants since they are slow growing, evergreen, available in a variety of forms and colours and require very little maintenance.

There are many different styles of kerbing or edging available. These must be set firmly into concrete so that they can withstand the pressure of car wheels.

These block paviors are interlocking so that they cannot easily move around after they have been set in position in a bed of sand or mortar.

It is important to set the outer row of blocks laterally so that they remain stable.

Drainage

Such a large area of paving, edged with a kerb, could flood in heavy rain, so you would have to ensure that its surface had an adequate 'fall', and install some form of drainage round the lowest edges to take the water away. In this garden, the paving slopes down to the road so that the water can flow away, but if the paving were to slope the other way, down to the house, drainage could be a serious problem.

To make sure you have the largest possible area of garden, the pedestrian area must be shaped carefully to ensure that it can be used to the full but does not have any more paving than is absolutely necessary. In this example, steps are needed up to the front door but these have been angled to make them approachable either from the car or from the road, and railings have been added for safety.

The slope of this garden has been partly terraced, mainly to create an upper level from which window cleaning can take place, but it has also provided the opportunity to build an attractive 'stone' wall with an interesting mock culvert. Once the paved surfaces and access points have been planned as economically as possible, the space left over will be available for garden although there will often be other considerations, such as the window cleaning access.

Here, the boundary walls have been given some attractive railings which might eventually be used to support some climbing plants. These are much more efficient in their use of space than hedges, and in a garden this small, with so much to accommodate, hedges would be a serious waste of space.

SEASONAL PLANTS

These seasonal flowers and bedding plants are particularly suitable for front parking lots. They will flower in shade, but not under trees.

Aubrieta and **spring-flowering bulbs**

Begonia semperflorens

Fuchsia

Impatiens (busy lizzie) – various colours

Linanthus – pink flowers in summer

Ornamental cabbages – coloured foliage

In addition to low-growing shrubs, pockets of dwarf spring flowers and alpines are useful for the sunnier edges.

Planting

Much of the garden can be planted in the same way as any other which is not specifically designed to accommodate a car. However, when it comes to planning for a variety of height and colour, with shrubs and herbaceous plants (and possibly a small tree or two), those areas immediately around the parking bay should have plants which will grow no higher than about 30cm (12in) so that car doors and the front of the car can pass over the top without any problems. Prickly plants such as roses, or anything which tends to topple and fall all over the place after heavy rain, such as *Lavatera*, should be kept well away from the parking and access area. Neat, low-growing plants providing all-the-year-round interest would be the ideal choice here, together with a few pots or tubs of seasonal flowers to brighten up odd corners. Plants grown in containers can be moved around, if necessary away from the car parking area if they grow too large.

It is often a good idea to 'soften' the house walls by planting some climbers and wall shrubs or merely by growing smaller plants along the bottom of the brickwork.

Garden seating

Creating somewhere to relax

In this easy-care garden, there are places both in the sun and in the shade to sit and relax.

Garden plan

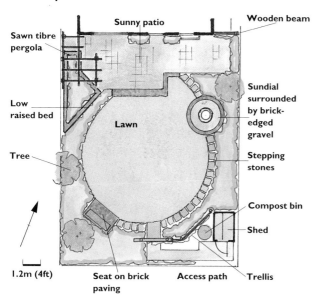

Sawn tibre pergola

Sunny patio

Wooden beam

Low raised bed

Sundial surrounded by brick-edged gravel

Lawn

Stepping stones

Tree

Compost bin

Shed

1.2m (4ft)

Seat on brick paving

Access path

Trellis

Seating has been arranged around this garden so that it will be possible to relax in either sun or shade.

Although garden benches are popular, a collection of individual seats can be particularly useful for social gatherings.

Whatever else you want from your garden, you are almost certain to want a special area for sitting out. The aspect of your garden will influence the position you choose for this, as most people would prefer to sit out of the wind and in the sun but, of course, on very hot days you might appreciate having somewhere to sit in the shade. If you are at work all day you will probably relax in the evening sunshine, but if you spend most of your time at home you will be able to sit in the sun more often and at different times of the day. Walking round your garden will soon reveal the best places for seating areas to meet your particular needs, even in gardens where there is only a little sun, although in such a situation your choices might be very limited. The various areas could range in size and complexity from full-size patios to smaller sheltered corners with just a modest garden seat, with plenty of alternative arrangements in between, depending upon how may people are likely to use them at any one time.

Siting a patio

The most obvious place for a patio is immediately out-side a door or French windows but if the sun never reaches those parts of your garden, it would probably be better to limit the area of paving there and build a full-sized patio elsewhere in the sunnier section. All sitting areas need a good degree of shelter, pleasant surroundings and an attractive outlook.

You might find that a patio constructed against the house can feel very bleak and isolated from the rest of the garden if there are no plants surrounding the area. Ideally, you should have planting around at least three sides of the patio which will mean having climbers up the walls and fences and some other planting at ground level. This will help to make anyone sitting there feel that they are actually within the garden and not on the edge of it.

You should make sure that your patio is shaped so that it can accommodate sufficient sun loungers, chairs or other garden furniture grouped in a sociable arrangement rather than all in a straight row. This will mean creating a larger area of paving in one place rather than having a strip, the same width, right across the back of the house. If you have a draughty passage-way along the side of the house, you could block it off with a solid gate; any lack of privacy on either side of your garden can be improved by the use of some screening and climbing plants.

A patio which is away from the house and further out in to the garden could well need screening on several sides, not just for privacy but also because it will be a much more restful place if it feels enclosed and protected. The positioning and fixing of a modest garden seat is obviously a much simpler matter than building a patio but even here it will feel more comfortable if you have tucked it into a corner or set it part way in to a mature border so that it is out of the wind and slightly secluded.

Smaller seating areas

An area which is smaller than a patio yet has more than just one seat can also be very useful and is more likely to be used by two or three people at a time of the day when light refreshments are needed. You might choose to position this type of feature to catch sun in mid-morning or in mid- to late afternoon or, alternatively, in a shady place as a refuge from the hot sun, since not everybody enjoys sitting in the sun. Arbours, gazebos and pergolas are all structures which cover a sitting area and provide various degrees of shade. They come in a variety of shapes: often round,

Stone seats are both attractive and virtually maintenance-free. Although they can be used as a brief resting place they tend not to be as comfortable as timber seating.

hexagonal or octagonal but sometimes square. In a small garden you would probably only have room for one of these structures.

An arbour

This is usually a metal (or timber) structure, perhaps large enough to seat two or three people. It would be almost completely covered by climbing plants and makes an ideal secluded retreat rather than a vantage point for looking out over spectacular views.

A gazebo

This is also made from metal or timber, will often be larger than an arbour and is sometimes elevated with several steps leading up into it. There may be a low wall or trellis around the bottom half, perhaps up to a height of 90cm (3ft) but it would accommodate fewer climbing plants and have relatively open sides. With its more open and less secluded aspect, you might position a gazebo to look out across the garden or surrounding countryside, particularly where the evening sunshine will fall. In a windy garden, you could add trellis covered with climbing plants to enclose some of the sides completely but this would reduce its panoramic vista. A gazebo will often be large enough to accommodate a garden table and chairs for snack meals and evening drinks.

Pergolas

There are two main types of pergola – the first can act as a covered walkway between two distinct areas of the garden, rather like a gazebo, usually incorporating a place to sit. A pergola will nearly always be constructed from timber rather than from metal and will often be of sawn timber rather than a 'rustic' construction. Unlike the gazebo, a pergola would usually be at ground level; the second is paved and large enough for some garden furniture. It could support a number of climbing plants and would therefore provide you with another shady place to sit. Unless your garden is very exposed or windy, you would normally leave the sides of a pergola completely open, often with access from several directions.

A view

Make sure that you position your sitting area so that it has a pleasant view out across the garden. A house, shed or garage without any planting in front of it or up its walls could be quite an eyesore when viewed

Most garden seating is placed on a hard surface which, though practical, can be rather stark especially in hot sunny weather. Pressure-treated timber decking, on the other hand, produces a more comfortable surface on which to arrange seating, and perhaps have children playing nearby.

from a seat, so bear in mind the different angles. You may find yourself having to reconsider the lay-out of the whole garden to avoid an unattractive situation such as this.

Paving

You could place a seat beneath a tree directly on the lawn but it may cause a nuisance during mowing. If you use the seat frequently, the lawn in front of it will soon wear out and become a muddy patch so, in most cases, a seat is better off on some form of paving. Shingle edged with brick, stone or timber provides a cheap solution and is preferable to grass or soil although it could kick out onto the surrounding lawn but there are, of course, many other forms of paving for you to choose which are attractive, stable and not necessarily always expensive. Shingle on the floor of a pergola or gazebo is not appropriate because of all the movement to and fro, so a more permanent form of paving, perhaps brick or stone, would be much more practical here.

Additional features

You can always turn a small sitting area into something more elaborate by introducing features usually associated with patios. A small pool with a fountain

For relaxing in the shade, what could be better than a seat around a tree together with a small amount of paving for wear and tear.

looks delightful, creates a feeling of cool freshness and, of course, provides the sound of trickling water, while a raised bed built at the back and on either side of a garden seat can help to produce the feeling of seclusion. Groups of tubs and pots can be used along with an ornament or two as focal points. For hot, sunny areas, a limited amount of pergola can be added to provide just a little shade at the hottest time of the day as well as providing an area for barbecue facilities and lighting for evening entertaining and sitting outside on warm summer evenings.

Planting

No sitting area can be complete without plants. Warm, sheltered corners will give you plenty of scope for introducing perfumed and aromatic plants and the still, warm air will encourage the fragrances to develop and linger. Colour, too, is important and this can often be provided by a selection of seasonal flowers and bulbs growing in tubs and pots. If there is a spot in the garden warm enough for you to sit out on a sunny winter's day, then shrubs with fragrant winter flowers, such as *Viburnum fragrans* and *Lonicera fragrantissima* would certainly be worth including.

You can vary the degree of shade your pergola affords by using different climbers. Those with rampant growth and large leaves, such as *Vitis coignetiae*, will produce dense shade while less vigorous climbers,

CLIMBING PLANTS FOR DENSE SHADE

Actinidia deliciosa
(Chinese gooseberry)

Aristolochia durior
(Dutchman's pipe)

Fallopia baldschuanica
(mile-a-minute vine)

Parthenocissus
(Virginia creeper)

Vitis coignetiae

Wisteria

Parthenocissus

A seat which is tucked in to some planting can feel cosier than one that stands out in the open, although the plants should be kept trimmed back from it.

A bench can have several temporary positions within a garden and be moved around to catch sun or shade at various times of the year.

such as honeysuckle and some clematis, would produce much lighter shade. In the garden illustrated here there are two distinct places to sit. The patio is in full sun for much of the day but, as the sun passes across and to the left, the pergola with its climbing plants should provide at least some protection from the hot afternoon sunshine. On very hot days, the garden seat on the edge of the lawn would be shaded by the tree just behind it and therefore provides a relatively cool place to sit.

Time to relax

This garden has been designed to require very little in the way of maintenance. The lawn has been shaped so that it is easy to mow, the stepping-stone path around the edge would help to keep its edges neat and allow easy access to all areas, and the borders are well stocked with plants so that weeding is kept to a minimum yet an attractive display is ensured.

FRAGRANT PLANTS

Corylopsis pauciflora
early spring

Chimonanthus praecox
(Winter sweet)

Choisya ternata
(Mexican orange blossom)

Daphne – various (these have poisonous berries)

Hamamelis
(witch hazel) in winter

Hyacinthus

Lilium regale and others

Lonicera halliana
(honeysuckle) and others

Jasminum officinale

Jasminum × stephanense

Mahonia most

Philadelphus

Roses – some but not all

Trachelospernum jasminoïdes –
a tender climber

Viburnums –
many

Choisya ternata 'Sundance'

Philadelphus coronarius

Garden case studies

Gardens can be designed for a wide range of activities, from hobby gardening to low maintenance plant tending and relaxation.

Secluded back garden

THE SITE

Dimensions – This rectangular garden is approximately 5 x 10m (16 x 33ft)

Aspect – The garden faces north, and the back of the house and the strip of garden immediately adjacent are always in the shade, but the rest of the plot is quite open and sunny

Soil type – The soil is fairly light and stony, with a neutral pH

Other information – The plot is pleasantly secluded, with a fence 1.8m (6ft) high on two sides and a 1.5m (5ft) high screen block wall on the left. There is an access path coming in from the right-hand side of the house and a gate in the top left-hand corner, connecting with the alleyway

The brief

This garden used to be about 90cm (3ft) shorter and 1.2m (4ft) narrower with an alleyway running down the right-hand side and across the end. An opportunity arose to buy the alleyway and incorporate it into the garden, making the plot longer and wider, but this has meant completely redesigning the whole garden. The new garden was to include some changes in level, more variation in the height of the planting and a more interesting selection of paving materials. There was to be a lion's head water feature spouting water into a small pool, a sitting-out area to accommodate some garden furniture, along with a portable gas barbecue and a good selection of plants including, if possible, one small tree. The existing garden shed could stay but access had to be retained to the gate in the top left-hand corner and to the path on the right-hand side of the house. The lay-out should also, if possible, have had some curves rather than consist solely of straight lines. The soil is quite light and well drained with a neutral pH.

Practicalities

The shed has been retained but tucked well in to the far right-hand corner where it can easily be concealed

Garden plan

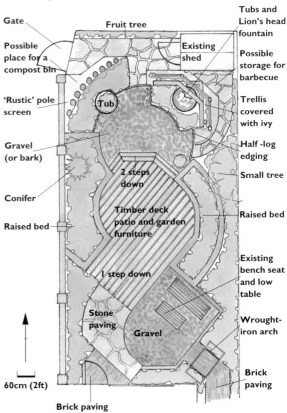

Gate · Fruit tree · Tubs and Lion's head fountain · Possible place for a compost bin · Existing shed · Possible storage for barbecue · 'Rustic' pole screen · Tub · Trellis covered with ivy · Gravel (or bark) · Half-log edging · 2 steps down · Small tree · Conifer · Timber deck patio and garden furniture · Raised bed · Raised bed · 1 step down · Existing bench seat and low table · Stone paving · Gravel · Wrought-iron arch · Brick paving · 60cm (2ft) · Brick paving

This is a low-maintenance garden which has a secluded timber deck. Various other types of paving have been included such as gravel and brick, together with a seat, an arch and an interesting and relaxing water feature. The planting is a mixture of shrubs and perennials which, together, will provide colour and foliage interest all the year round. Any unsightly features have been concealed behind trellis and climbing plants.

from sight and will not take up too much space. Some trellis has been fixed to the side of the shed and a small area in front of this, sectioned off with trellis and planting, provides somewhere to keep the barbecue or a compost bin out of sight. There is a narrow paved access to the left-hand gate but this has been screened with an arrangement of heavy 'rustic' poles, partly covered by climbing plants.

THE NEW DESIGN

The sunbathing and dining area

The back of the house is in shade, so the main sun-bathing area has had to be positioned further into the garden. With a 'see-through' screen block wall only 1.5m (5 ft) high to the left, it has been a priority to create at least a degree of privacy and seclusion round the sunbathing area. This has been achieved, in part, by introducing some curved raised beds and planting which will grow high enough to provide the privacy required without blocking out sunlight or offending the neighbours.

Timber decking has been used as flooring between these beds and has been raised by about 15cm (6in) to provide the change in level. With the beds raised about 38cm (15in) higher than this, the whole central part of the garden will feel comfortable to sit in and will be at a significantly different height to the rest of the garden.

The timber decking is easier to install than most other types of paving; it feels warmer and, comparatively speaking, is not particularly expensive. It has been supported on a series of strong joists closely spaced so that the planks or 'floor boards' cannot spring or warp. These planks must have gaps of about 1cm (⅜in) left between them so that water can drain away and not make them slippery in winter. All the timber in this project has been pressure treated against decay and stained a soft chocolate brown.

Decking is especially useful in a small garden where a lawn might not be practical. It can be arranged in various patterns and stained an attractive colour.

A sunny and secluded garden

Both the planting and the materials used are of mainly soft colours to produce a relaxing atmosphere.

Walling and paving

Although the house is built of bricks, it was decided to use natural stone for the raised beds, since this would create a softer visual effect. At the same time, some climbing plants have been grown up the rear wall of the house so that its appearance is softened and the brickwork is much less obvious. To go with the stone, between the house and the deck is a small area of stone crazy paving but a step, immediately outside the French windows, and a small section of path leading from the side passageway have been built in brick because they are virtually joined to the house. There is a little more crazy paving at the far end of the garden, leading to the shed and corner gate but this has been used to avoid having to cut paving slabs or bricks to fit around the rather complicated shape rather than for aesthetic reasons.

The rest of the 'hard' surfaces are in a brown gravel (not shingle) and edged, where necessary, with some strips of half-log edging. The small area of gravel close to the house has been chosen as the site of a garden

Curves and winding paths together with small changes in level will help to produce an intimate garden although it takes several years to achieve seclusion using plants.

Sometimes partial seclusion, like that provided by this wrought-iron gate, is more appropriate and less likely to feel stifling than the dense screening from a fence and climbers.

seat and table (both with wrought-iron legs). These would not catch a lot of sun until high summer but they do provide somewhere to sit, close to the house, for a short rest. It will also provide somewhere to place a laundry basket while hanging out washing; a hole and socket for the rotary washing line have been built in to the centre of the timber deck in case one is ever needed later.

Special features
The passageway leading down the side of the house is

not particularly attractive so an elegant iron rose arch has been placed across this corner as both an entrance to the garden and a partial screen to the passageway. The climbers on the arch need not, of course, be roses; fragrant climbers like *Jasminum officinale* (summer jasmine) and *Lonicera* (honeysuckle) would be equally suitable. This wrought-iron arch, the table and the seat were all chosen to match.

'Zéphyrine Drouhin' is a thornless rose which will quickly cover the top section of a fence or screen.

A wall fountain

The sound of trickling water from this fountain will create a relaxing atmosphere and temper the heat of a summer's day.

The lion's head water feature has been built in to a special timber wall rather than in to brick or stonework, partly to reduce the cost but also for ease of construction. The timber wall is made from 10cm (4in) thick strips of timber. This had recently been pressure treated, so it was allowed to dry out thoroughly before being sealed with a water-repellent stain. Without this, some of the pressure-treatment chemical could possibly have been washed out by heavy rain and would have poisoned the water in the small pool below. The lion's head is suspended right over a large wooden tub which has been set down into the ground (within a continuous sheet of polythene) as a pool. This positioning will ensure that, even on a windy day, the water from the lion's mouth will go in to the pool and not blow too far off course. An electricity supply and a submersible pump to circulate the water have been installed by a qualified electrician.

Planting

Plants have had to be chosen carefully for this garden so that they produce the right effect. Planting around the front of the water feature, for example, has been selected to be low-growing, to associate well with water and not conceal the attractive, rounded cobble stones. A number of dwarf ornamental grasses and bamboos have been included along with some small primulas and a few *Erica carnea* (winter-flowering heathers).

Apart from the mainly shrubby plants used either side of the decking to provide some privacy, there are various shrubs, a tree and some herbaceous flowering plants which provide the required variation in height and some winter interest. The rear fence is in full sun much of the time and has therefore been planted with a fan-trained fruit tree. It would also be possible to grow some strawberries in a large tub or pot, have hanging baskets of trailing tomatoes and possibly even beans growing over the arch as a way of producing some food in a very confined space.

CARPETING PLANTS FOR GRAVEL

The following plants can be used as carpeting plants in areas of gravel, but you will have to hand-weed around them rather than use herbicides:

***Acaena microphylla* 'Pulchella'**
Bronze foliage and reddish-brown flowers in late summer. Height 10cm (4in).

***Ajuga reptans* 'Braunherz'**
Glossy, deep purple foliage and spikes of blue flowers in summer. Height 15cm (6in).

Campanula pulla
Creeping stems carry violet-purple, bell-shaped flowers during summer. Height 5cm (2in).

***Chamaemelum nobile* 'Treneague'**
A non-flowering form of camomile forming mats of green, mossy, aromatic foliage. Height 15cm (6in).

Dryas octopetala
Mats of greyish-green foliage and white flowers during summer. Height 5cm (2in).

Polygonum vaccinifolium
Mats of green foliage turn a rich brown in autumn. Masses of pink flower spikes produced in late summer. Height 15cm (6in).

Saxifraga

Saxifraga
All the mossy saxifrages would be suitable as long as the soil is not constantly wet or shaded. Average height 10cm (4in)

Sempervivum (houseleek)
All are suitable. Average height when in flower 10cm (4in)

Thymus serpyllum
(prostrate thyme)
This and various other thymes would be suitable. Many have interesting foliage and masses of mainly pink or purple flowers. Height 5cm (2in)

Sempervivum

Patio garden

The brief

The garden has been designed for a young, working couple who enjoy gardening and eating outdoors but do not have a lot of spare time to spend looking after their garden. Their new garden lay-out was to include a patio area for eating out, space for a rotary washing line, somewhere to sit and an attractive area of paving right across the back of the house to provide access. The car parking area was to be improved and space provided for an ugly green wheeled bin, and a compost bin. If possible there should be one or two interesting features perhaps including some water, somewhere to store pots, tools and compost, to take cuttings and to sow seeds. The planting should include attractive shrubs, herbaceous and seasonal flowers as well as space for a few vegetables and some soft fruit.

Practicalities

The first task has been to find a home for the compost and wheeled bins, both of which can be smelly in hot weather. The best solution has been to tuck them

Garden plan

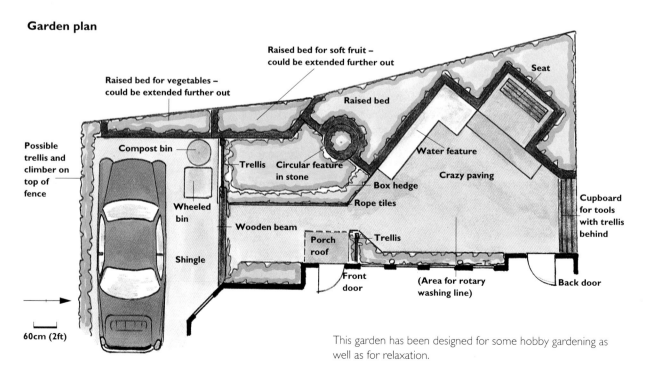

This garden has been designed for some hobby gardening as well as for relaxation.

behind a planted 'rustic' trellis screen at the narrowest end of the garden near the car. The wheeled bin would be easy to roll out from here and down the short driveway to the roadside. The planted trellis has been fixed onto one side of an arch which has been made from two uprights, a cross-beam and two ornate metal brackets so that, together, they partly separate the car parking and utility area from the rest of the garden. Another small section of 'rustic' trellis, projecting a short distance from the right-hand side of the porch (see plan) helps to keep the main patio area at least partly screened from visitors using the front door. The main garden lies between the wooden arch and the right-hand boundary, which is a low brick wall topped with some more 'rustic' trellis and climbing plants. This not only hides the ugly shed next door but provides a degree of privacy and seclusion.

Every effort has been made throughout the garden to use materials which are sympathetic to the age of the house and appropriate to its style, although stone has been used rather than brick to produce a more antiquated effect.

A patio can sometimes seem rather harsh unless it is given an interesting shape and some additional features. Its edges should also be partially hidden by overflowing plants.

A front and back garden combined

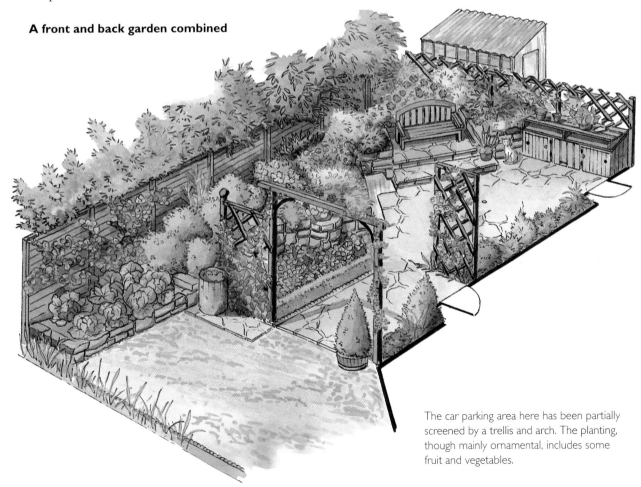

The car parking area here has been partially screened by a trellis and arch. The planting, though mainly ornamental, includes some fruit and vegetables.

THE NEW DESIGN

Raised beds

The bank which runs along the back of the plot is at
its highest at the right-hand end so the stone raised
beds have been designed to accommodate this. At the
car park end, the raised bed is considerably lower and
acts more as a kerb for the parked car.

Focal features

Care has had to be taken not to have too many different features cluttering up the limited space available,
yet at the same time produce an interesting garden.
The low raised bed at the front of the parked car has
been planted with a few vegetables which should
thrive despite the proximity of some overhanging
trees and shrubs. This bed could be extended outwards a little further, but not too far otherwise it
would begin to reduce the area available for car parking. To the right of this is another, slightly higher
raised bed planted with some bush fruit.

Opposite the front door is a small bed at ground
level which has been edged with *Buxus* (box) and some
Victorian rope-edge tiles. This bed has been planted
up with strawberries but it could just as easily have
accommodated more vegetables instead. Behind is a
higher raised bed which comes in at an angle from the
right. This really signifies the beginning of the ornamental part of the garden and, consequently, contains
a good selection of mainly shrubby and trailing plants.
Apart from being at an angle, the retaining wall of this
bed has been built with a circular feature which

Apart from its attractive appearance, a small fountain also
provides the sound of water which can be very soothing. In
winter the running water may help to prevent the pond from
freezing over.

amounts to a stone shelf where an attractive bowl of
seasonal flowers can be stood. All these walls are holding back quite a lot of soil so they are at least 21.5cm
(8½in) thick and have weepholes to allow water
to pass through.

Seating area

As the garden widens a little, so the retaining walls
have been moved back to create a paved area where
some garden furniture could be arranged for outdoor
meals, or a washing line erected. Although there is not
a lot of space here, it did seem worth giving up some
of the potential planting space to add a small raised
platform and a garden seat which can be used even
when the main area of paving is not in use as a patio.
A slightly dated looking seat has been used to keep
things in an antiquated style.

A patio garden would not be complete without a collection of
pots for seasonal flowers.

Victorian rope-edged tiles make an ideal border, preventing soil
from washing down onto the paving.

The water feature

This has been designed as a fast-flowing gully which disappears beneath the retaining wall facing the house. A pump has been placed under here to take water and circulate it through a hidden pipe in to the opposite end of the feature so that water appears to flow from one end to the other like a stream. The pump is quite a powerful one and the stream or gully has been lined with round cobble stones so that, when the water is moving at a good speed, it makes a pleasant gurgling sound. There are no fish in here but there are some aquatic plants.

A 'fold-away' cupboard

With no grass, there is no need for a mower but there are various other garden tools which have to be stored. A special storage cupboard has been built to fit in to a gap just to the right of the back door and up against the boundary wall. Although its top has a sloping roof to shed rainwater, a slatted shelf has been built above it. The cupboard has three stout wooden doors with the centre one flapping up so that it can be supported by the other two and become a small potting bench. The slatted top shelf will be useful during potting sessions but, at other times, could accommodate various pots and boxes of seasonal flowers. All the timber has been pressure treated to protect it from decay.

Planting

Apart from the small areas of soft fruit and vegetables, the planting is ornamental with a predominance of shrubs along the rear boundary under the overhanging trees. Away from these trees and towards the front of the raised beds in the seating area, a number of small shrubs and shrubby herbs with coloured foliage have been interspersed with trailing plants and seasonal bedding. There is a selection of climbers on the various sections of trellis, and some pots of flowers in odd corners. Eventually, some hanging baskets will be hung from the arch and the house walls to complete the 'all-round' planting in this unusual patio garden.

PLANTS FOR PATIOS

Small ground-level flower beds, along with the relatively high raised beds, can become quite dry, especially during summer, so plants should be chosen with this in mind.

Alchemilla mollis (lady's mantle)
Feathery sprays of greeny-yellow flowers in mid-summer

Berberis
Deciduous varieties have yellow flowers from late spring to early summer followed by coloured berries and autumn foliage

Bergenia
Excellent ground cover with large, evergreen, glossy leaves and flowers from early to late spring.

***Cistus* 'Silver Pink'**
Evergreen shrub with saucer-shaped, clear pink flowers in the summer

***Escallonia* 'Apple Blossom'**
Evergreen, bushy shrub with pale pink flowers early to mid-summer

Bergenia cordifolia

Hebe
Any of the smaller, small-leaf types are suitable

***Potentilla fruticosa* 'Elizabeth'**
Deciduous, bushy shrub with bright yellow flowers late spring to mid-autumn. *P. f.* 'Red Ace' has stunning vermillion flowers

Salvia (sage)
Aromatic foliage and year-round colour

Santolina chamaecyparissus nana (cotton lavender)
Silver, aromatic foliage. Profuse yellow, button-shaped flowers in summer

Santolina chamaecyparissus

'Stock' brick or black paviors can be laid to various patterns. This one is called a basket weave.

Modern cottage garden

THE SITE

Dimensions – This garden is about 10 x 16m (33ft x 52ft)

Aspect – The back of the house is in constant shade, but the rest of the garden is quite sunny, despite all the overgrown boundary planting

Soil type – The soil is alkaline and rather heavy but, away from the conifer, quite fertile. The soil is quite heavy with some clay; it is alkaline with a high pH value

Other information – This overgrown garden is at the back of an older chalet bungalow. The owners have been busy clearing waist-high weeds and have found the remnants of an old stone path and various mature shrubs. There is a rather overgrown conifer hedge down the left-hand side and a row of overgrown conifers and scrub on the right. The end section of the plot is actually a car park and is partly separated from the garden by an existing ivy-covered arch and a short section of wall. At the back of the house not far from the right-hand corner and the side passageway is a messy looking shed with a little extension on the back. There is a semi-mature apple tree in what used to be the lawn and a small Christmas tree near the car park

Garden plan

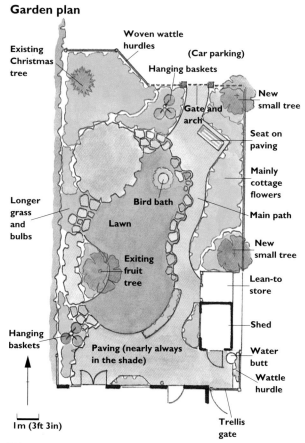

This garden is a compromise between a cottage garden, which would normally require quite a lot of maintenance, and a modern low-maintenance garden which has to cope with a good deal of family activity.

Labels: Existing Christmas tree; Woven wattle hurdles; (Car parking); Hanging baskets; New small tree; Gate and arch; Seat on paving; Mainly cottage flowers; Main path; Bird bath; Longer grass and bulbs; Lawn; New small tree; Lean-to store; Exiting fruit tree; Shed; Hanging baskets; Water butt; Paving (nearly always in the shade); Wattle hurdle; Trellis gate

1m (3ft 3in)

The brief

The new design for the garden is to enable it to look as much like a cottage garden as possible. It should have a paved area, preferably down towards the car park which is in the sun, a seat and a herbaceous border. Although the finished garden should not look too tidy and organized, it must be reasonably easy to look after. Most of the old stone path should be restored and extended in a similar style but be smooth and wide enough for everyday use and for a pram. Some form of screening is needed to prevent passers-by walking along in front of the bungalow and seeing the tatty shed at the garden end of the side passage. The shed itself needs a face-lift. The left-hand row of conifers has to stay but all the plants on the right can come out and be replaced by some sort of new

boundary. There should be space for a rotary washing line, and the garden to the left of the existing arch and wall could be extended a little further back into the car park area.

Practicalities

The top priority has been to make sure that the route between the house and the cars will stand up to everyday use in all weathers. A sunny patio, borders for plenty of cottage-garden plants and a more attractive shed also came high on the priority list.

A cottage garden

Wherever possible, edges have been softened and cottage-garden flowers used to create a colourful and informal effect.

THE NEW DESIGN

Compromise

Not all aspects of a true cottage garden are compatible with busy modern life so some compromises have had to be made. The present (existing) path up to the car park might look very attractive, with odd-shaped stone slabs set into the soil and wide, grassy gaps between, but would hardly be easy to push a pram across in winter and one day it might be needed for a tricycle and other toys. The compromise has been to construct a normal stone crazy-paving path, pointed and with a relatively straight edge down the right-hand side, but an apparently fragmented one on the left, alongside part of the lawn. This left-hand side is also constructed as a normal crazy-paving path but all the materials

have had to be cut off cleanly so that soil and grass can grow right up to it. Individual pieces of paving have then been set into the grass, close to the edge of the new path to reproduce, at least in part, a modified version of the old, stepping-stone path.

Another, narrower path has been constructed alongside the conifer screen on the left to allow easy maintenance. This is a mixture of stepping stones set in the grass, with some short sections of the solid but ragged-edged crazy paving. The almost circular patio has also been constructed from this ragged-edged paving so that, overall, the effect is quite informal, and comes close to the traditional cottage-garden effect.

A sunny border

The rather untidy and overgrown trees and shrubs down the right-hand side have been taken out and replaced by 1.2m (4ft) high woven hazel (wattle) hurdles or panels set between and wired onto 'rustic' poles. This not only looks 'cottagey' but is also useful for supporting some climbing plants. Between this fence and the new path is a new sunny border which has been planted mainly with traditional herbaceous flowers. A similar style of fence has been used around the new small piece of garden which was previously part of the car park, but this one is 1.8m (6ft) high.

Face lift

The tatty old shed has been given a complete face-lift and the extension on the back completely rebuilt. The shed originally had a window which was about 45cm (18in) deep and ran the whole length of one side. The two end sections of this window have been panelled over with vertical strips of pine which go from just under the eaves right down to the ground. This has left the two remaining centre sections of the window and the original, horizontal shed panelling under-neath, unaffected. Diamond trellis has been fixed onto the two sections of pine panelling, onto the original panelling around the door and onto the side of the new extension. The roof has been re-felted and given new, more generous gables and the remaining sections

This valuable carpeting plant, *Anthemis punctata* ssp. *cupaniana*, will spill over rocks and the edge of paths.

of window have been fitted with a curved fillet of wood at the top. A window box has been added for some seasonal bedding and a *Clematis* 'Jackmanii' trained up the side and onto the roof. This provides colour and camouflage at the same time.

Patio door paving

Although the back of the bungalow is always in shade, there is still access onto the area through some French windows, so it has been necessary to pave quite a generous area to provide a link with the shed, the side passage and the path to the car park. The permanent planting around here is not likely to be particularly colourful but a post to support hanging baskets of flowers has been fixed on the left-hand side to brighten up the view from the French windows. Another, similar post with more baskets has been fixed in to a border next to the arched gate, and a rotary washing line socket in to a cluster of stone slabs flush with the lawn.

New gates

The ivy-covered brick pillar and arch have been left much as they were but a new picket gate and fence have been fitted to match the overall cottage-garden style. To the side of the bungalow, a strong, hinged trellis gate, supporting a honeysuckle, has been fitted across the passageway to hide the shed from passers-by. All the timberwork in the garden must be well protected from pests and decay, and stained the same colour throughout so that it all matches. This will give the garden a sense of unity.

Picket fencing comes in a variety of styles, all of which blend in well with cottage gardens.

This seat set among informal planting beside a gravel path is typical of a cottage garden.

Planting

A collection of shrubs including the Christmas tree and a few border flowers have been planted in part of the garden that used to be the car park, with climbing plants on the wattle fencing behind. Apart from these shrubs, no plants have been planted directly up against the left-hand conifers because of the difficult growing conditions. Planting in the small beds against the back of the bungalow has been chosen to be especially shade tolerant and includes *Iris foetidissima* (grown for its scarlet seeds), *Viburnum davidii* and *Euonymus fortunei* 'Emerald Gaiety'. A short hedge of *Lavandula augustifolia* 'Hidcote' separates the lawn from the paving just outside the shed and some bulbs have been planted in the grass around the bird bath.

The fruit tree has been retained and incorporated into a border of mainly low-growing shrubs and herbaceous flowers, including *Spiraea japonica* 'Gold Flame' (golden foliage) and *Geranium* 'Johnson's Blue', a herbaceous geranium with blue flowers. Although the new border to the left of the garden path contains mostly herbaceous flowers, a small tree, *Prunus* × *blireiana*, and an evergreen shrub, *Elaeagnus* × *ebbingii*, have been planted as a screen at the car park end, and another tree, *Sorbus* 'Joseph Rock', a mountain ash, and the evergreen *Viburnum tinus* have been planted at the opposite end against the shed extension. Some herbs have been included in some of the borders together with various other aromatic plants, and clusters of crocuses have been planted under the lawn to provide some colour in the early spring. These bulbs will require patches of grass to be left uncut for a few

COTTAGE-GARDEN STYLE PLANTS

Even in a modern setting, it is possible to create a cottage-garden effect by choosing flowers with an informal, old-fashioned look. Here are some suitable plants that also perform well:

Alchemilla mollis (lady's mantle)
Clump-forming perennial with feathery sprays of tiny, green-yellow flowers in mid-summer

Aquilegia (granny's bonnet, columbine)
A cottage-garden favourite with bell-shaped flowers in shades of blue, pink, white and yellow

Aquilegia

Buddleia (butterfly bush)
Fast-growing shrub with small clusters of mostly purple or mauve flowers in summer

Campanula (bellflower)
Cottage-garden plants *par excellence*

Ceanothus 'Autumnal Blue'
Evergreen, bushy shrub with clusters of pale blue flowers

Dianthus (pinks)
Excellent for cutting; grey, grass-like foliage present all year. Flowers fragrant

Campanula

Echinacea purpurea 'Robert Bloom' (purple coneflower)
Deep crimson-pink, daisy-like flowers with brown centres on very long stems

Helleborus (Christmas or Lenten rose)
Evergreen foliage, large, saucer-shaped flowers in winter and spring

Lupinus (lupin)
Long spikes of pea-like flowers in wide variety of colours, produced in summer

Myrtus communis (common myrtle)
Evergreen, bushy shrub with fragrant, white flowers followed by berries

Lupinus

Papaver somniferum (opium poppy)
Large, papery flowers in shades of red, pink, purple or white borne in summer

Philadelphus (mock orange)
Summer-flowering shrub with many fragrant, white, single or double flowers

Phlox
Annual and perennial forms available in wide range of colours

weeks while their foliage dies back, making the lawn look more informal and less manicured than a standard suburban lawn.

Sloping front garden

THE SITE

Dimensions – The garden measures about 7.2m (24ft) across from right to left (as far as the driveway) and about 3.6m (12ft) from the house down to the pavement, but there is an extra piece of land going just beyond the right-hand end of the house

Aspect – The garden faces south and is in full sun nearly all day

Soil type – The soil is very poor and is full of builders' rubble

Other information – This modern, detached house belongs to a young couple who are out at work all day. It has been built into sloping land, so the front garden drops away to the pavement by about 75cm (2ft 6in). There are three drains at the right-hand end of the plot

The brief

The garden must be as attractive and colourful as possible but easy to maintain. Access to the front door is to be improved so that the postman (and other visitors) does not have to cut across the garden to make his deliveries, and more paving is needed outside the front door so that guests have somewhere to stand while they are waiting to enter.

Practicalities

A flat garden is easier to look after than a sloping one, so both lay-outs have been conceived around some form of terracing, which would provide several small flat areas. Because the soil was full of rubble, it would have been necessary to dig it away whatever the style of garden, so building the terracing has not involved very much more excavation.

Although bricks have been used in the first scheme, illustrated here, the amount of brickwork needed was not very great so costs have not been especially high. The second scheme shows how terracing could have been done with vertical poles which, although not as permanent, cost less and are easier to use than bricks and concrete.

Garden plan

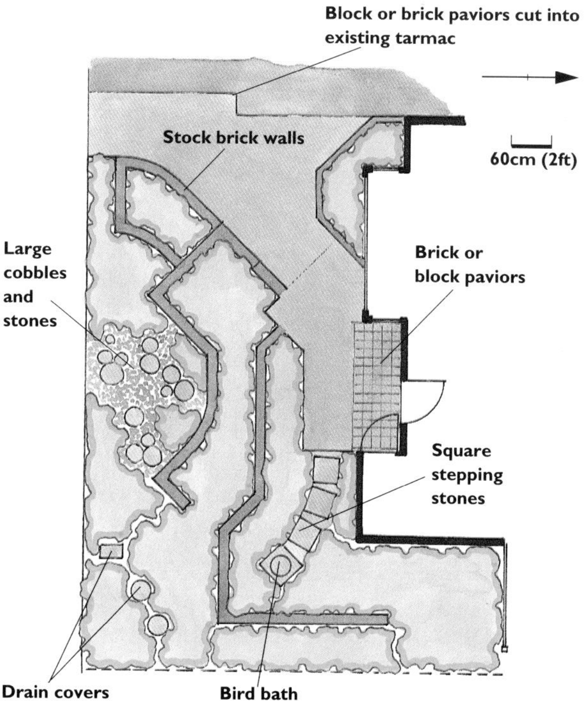

Perhaps the most important aspect of a front garden is a generous route to the front door to avoid taking short cuts across the garden itself.

THE NEW DESIGN

Designing out the problems

The first scheme illustrated here solves the problem of the postman taking a short cut by providing a wider, more direct route to the front door, together with a larger area of paving outside the front door itself where visitors can stand comfortably without falling back into the plants. There are many different types of paving materials which could have been used here – square or random rectangular slabs laid at an angle of either 45° or 90° to the house and edged with stock bricks (or block paviors), black (or red) tarmac with the same type of edging or, as shown here, brick-coloured block paviors laid to a basket-weave pattern.

A practical yet attractive lay-out

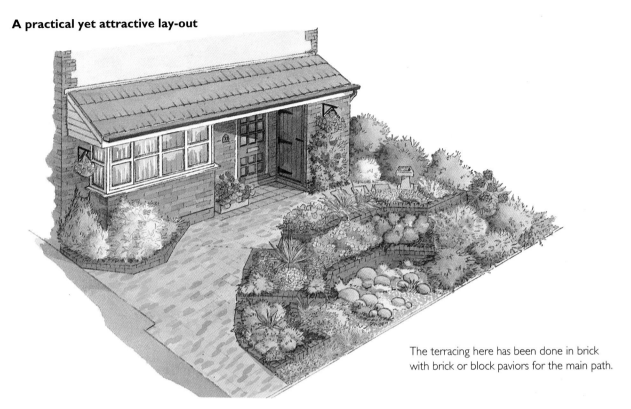

The terracing here has been done in brick with brick or block paviors for the main path.

Terracing

The retaining walls only terrace about two-thirds of this garden. The lower area has been left mainly as a slope, except for a small section in the middle which has been cut back level with the pavement. The presence of the three drain covers at the right-hand end of the plot have been the main reason for not terracing this lower area.

The first job was to dig away a lot of the soil and put in the concrete foundations for the walls, starting at the edge of the pavement and working back. A small amount of good topsoil was separated from the rubble and kept on one side. The walls are about 21.5cm (8½in) thick with all the visible portions in stock brick and the back in 10cm (4in) thick concrete blocks, to save money. A few weepholes were left here and there, close to the bottom of each wall to prevent water from building up behind.

Apart from the area of paving outside the front door, this terracing has produced a small, level upper garden with stepping stones leading to a bird bath. The next terrace down is also level but stops short at the right-hand end so that the original slope can remain much as it was, to leave the three drains undisturbed. There is another small terrace alongside the lower part of the driveway, to provide it with some structural stability and act as a kerb. The small section alongside the pavement was dug out a little way and filled with the saved topsoil. Some large rounded boulders have been arranged in groups, with a number of alpines planted between them and a mulch of gravel put over any remaining bare soil.

The subsoil in the bottom of the two main terraces was dug over and then both were filled (and compacted) to within about 1cm (⅜in) of the top with good quality, medium-loam topsoil. A problem with

Steps should, if possible, be shallow and wide enough for at least two people to walk side by side.

beds formed in this way is that, in time, the soil sinks and any prostrate plants which were intended to grow straight out and down over the sides, end up having to grow up the inside wall of the bed before they can grow over the top. In this garden, the topsoil was added in layers about 10cm (4in) deep and compacted each time. If the layers had been over-compacted, planting might have been difficult and poor drainage would have caused problems for the new planting. The bed against the bay window was constructed and filled at about the same time as the rest.

The paving

All the stock brick edges and a compacted base of scalpings were put down early on in the job, but the actual surface of block paviors, which were vibrated down onto a bed of sand, was not added until the terraces were complete (but not planted). For a week or two, visitors had to walk across planks lying on top of the scalpings. Walking directly on top of scalpings can lead to white (or reddish-brown) dust and grime being carried into the house on people's shoes.

A disc cutter was hired to cut a precise line through the existing black tarmac and this sharp edge was protected and treated very carefully right up until the moment when the block paviors were laid up against it. This meant that no extra tarmac was needed at the end of the job for patching and repairing.

The timber version

The poles used in the alternative lay-out can be bought milled so that they are the same diameter top and bottom. They will have been pressure treated and therefore be pale green but could be stained before use. Ideally, they should be inserted into the ground by as much as they protrude above it (soil conditions permitting) and never less than 30cm (1ft), even for the shortest ones. The bank would have to be 'stripped out' as before and those walls nearest the pavement constructed first. Whereas the brick walls have acted as an edge to the new paving, these poles would not be firm enough so, ideally, the paving would be laid quite independently from these log retaining walls.

Since the foundation for the paving will extend a little beyond its surface with some mortar haunching along the edges, the poles are likely to end up several centimetres (an inch or so) away from the edge of the paving. This gap could be filled with sharp sand or gravel. Although the poles will have been put very

An alternative lay-out

Here, terracing has been achieved using heavy-duty vertical poles set deep in to the ground.

firmly into the ground there is a risk that they might be pushed forward. This can be minimized by wiring them together across the back with stout, galvanized fencing wire and staples to hold the wire in place.

Planting

Plants (for the brick version) were chosen for their summer flowers and included *Potentilla fruticosa* 'Elizabeth', (yellow flowers) and *Caryopteris* **x** *clandonensis* blue flowers, *Cistus* 'Silver Pink', (pink flowers), and *Hydrangea involucrata* 'Hortensis', (pink). Others were chosen for their bright or coloured foliage, including *Salvia officinalis* 'Purpurascens' (purple-leaves), *Lavandula*

Steps which are set in to a bank will benefit from generous planting either side.

Garden plan

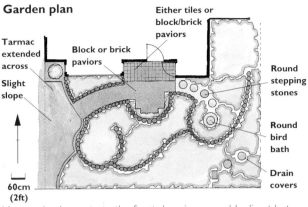

Tarmac extended across

Slight slope

Block or brick paviors

Either tiles or block/brick paviors

Round stepping stones

Round bird bath

Drain covers

60cm (2ft)

Here again, the route to the front door is reasonably direct but with a different paving arrangement.

'Hidcote' (silvery foliage), and *Santolina chamaecyparissus* (white leaves). A number of evergreen shrubs have been included for winter interest along with a couple of yuccas, the alpines and pockets of seasonal bedding plants. Several trailing plants have been used over the retaining walls, including *Cotoneaster dammeri* var. *radicans* (small, evergreen leaves and red berries), *Ajuga reptans* 'Braunherz' (dark purple leaves), *Lysimachia nummularia* 'Aurea' (golden trailing stems) and some *Cerastium Tomentosum* (grey leaves and white flowers). These terraces will become very dry during the summer and will need watering. After a year or so, the soil will need topping up with nutrients and this can be done either with a granular or a liquid balanced feed containing nitrogen, phosphates, trace elements and potash (N.P.K.). If the imported topsoil was free from perennial weeds, maintenance should be easy.

There are many suitable highly colourful plants, including seasonal bedding which will thrive in a sunny garden.

PLANTS FOR RAISED BEDS

The following plants are, in the main, slow-growing and therefore ideal for this kind of garden design, as they will not smother or undermine the retaining walls:

Azalea
Some of the smaller types would be useful on the upper terraces

Berberis thunbergii 'Atropurpurea Nana'
Dwarf, rounded habit and purple-red foliage

Buxus (box)
Must be kept clipped

Ceanothus thyrsiflorus repens
Evergreen, forming a wide, spreading mat covered with blue flowers in spring

Cordyline australis
Useful as a dot plant, but slightly tender

Cotoneaster dammeri 'Oakwood'
A ground-hugging type

Cytisus x beanii and **C. kewensis**
Yellow flowers on arching stems, eventually 30cm (12in) high

Erica carnea (winter-flowering heather)
Lime tolerant and mat-forming

Euonymus fortunei radicans
Evergreen shrubs, many cultivars, all ground-hugging

Hebe 'Youngii' and **H. pimeleoides 'Quicksilver'**
Rounded, evergreen flowering shrubs eventually reaching 30cm (12in) or so

Hedera helix 'Buttercup' (ivy)
Useful ground cover. Bright green leaves turn rich yellow in full sun

Ilex crenata 'Golden Gem' (holly)
Small, golden leaves. Eventually reaches 40cm (16in) or so

Lavandula angustifolia 'Hidcote' (lavender)
Aromatic, evergreen, silver-grey foliage and rich purple-blue flower spikes

Leucothoe 'Scarletta'
Prefers partial shade and bears attractive, white flowers

Pachysandra terminalis 'Variegata'
Creeping perennial with clusters of cream-variegated leaves

Leucothoe 'Scarletta'

Rhododendron impeditum
Varieties with mostly purple-blue flowers, may reach 40cm (16in)

Rosmarinus officinalis Prostratus Group (rosemary)
Almost prostrate but slightly tender

Salix alpina (willow)
Fairly prostrate with catkins in spring

Santolina chamaecyparissus nana (cotton lavender)
Aromatic, silvery foliage and yellow, button-like flowers

Vaccinium vitis-idaea
Evergreen, prostrate shrub, prefers humus-rich, semi-shaded conditions

Yucca filamentosa
Ideal dot plants, particularly variegated forms

Plant-lover's garden

The brief

The garden has been designed for a very keen gardener who wants to grow as wide a range of plants as possible and is prepared to spend a good deal of time in the garden. The owner recently moved from a much larger garden and has brought a collection of plants with her, including some trees and a number of shrubs, so there must be room to accommodate them. Apart from the trees and shrubs, the owner would like a bog garden to accommodate moisture-loving plants, a pool for water subjects, a scree bed for alpines, as much border space as possible for herbaceous plants, and fences, trelliswork and arches for climbing plants. There must also be space to grow a large collection of bulbs scattered in amongst the different beds, keeping the alpine bulbs to the scree bed. Despite all the gardening activity, there must also be somewhere to relax.

Practicalities

There are a number of essential, practical considerations to be taken into account. Firstly, the new garden design has to work around the well-established climbers and hedges, which must be left much as they are to ensure a degree of privacy. Ideally, the owner would also like some way of framing the fine view out over the countryside to draw more attention to it. The field beyond does, however, contain rabbits, moles

Garden plan

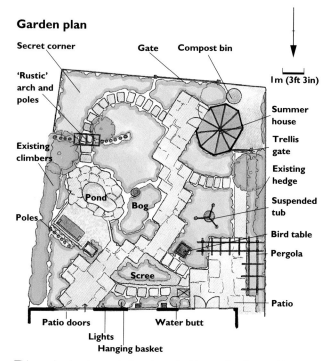

This garden has been designed as a hobby garden for a wide range of plants.

and sometimes deer, all of which must be kept out of the garden if the plants are to survive. There is an octagonal summer house, with good views over the fields, which has to stay where it is and will be incorporated into the new design. There should also be some paving outside the patio doors for reasons of access, but this does not necessarily mean a full-sized patio. The owners have built a garden room on the south-west corner of the house and so a small patio area outside this would be useful on warm sunny days, along with some form of path to connect both paved areas with the summer house.

THE NEW DESIGN

Protective fencing

Chicken wire, with a maximum mesh gauge of 3.5cm (1½in), has been introduced along the boundaries on the outside of the garden. This new fence is about

There is no grass in this garden, but stone paths provide a route through various types of planting.

45cm (18in) high, with 15cm (6in) buried in the ground to keep out the rabbits. Not only will this fence protect the garden from unwanted wildlife but, at the same time, it can hardly be seen from the garden and so will not detract from the view.

Another likely invasion from the field is weeds and, although not much can be done about migrating seeds apart from regular weeding, a physical barrier made of 1000-gauge PVC sheeting put 45cm (18in) vertically down into the ground has been installed to help prevent the spread of perennial weeds with creeping roots, such as couch grass, ground elder and perhaps even the seemingly unstoppable bindweed. This barrier will also help to keep out moles.

Framing the view
The existing rear boundary bordering the field consisted of a mixture of horizontal wood planks and wire. Although it was possible to see through and over

this, it did partially obscure the view, so the new design incorporates a non-opening, metal, five-bar gate. This looks more attractive than the fence and allows a much better view.

Garden lay-out
With so much demand on space for planting, garden features and paths, there is simply no room for a lawn as well. The lay-out of the paths must, therefore, be flexible but is fairly complex as it must allow easy access to all the borders. The main slant of the hard landscaping in the new design is diagonal, for a square layout would have made the garden look smaller that it really is, as well as being too rigid. The diagonal approach provides a more flexible and useful space overall, and helps to make a more natural vista from the patio doors across to the field gate.

Making one or two of the paths curved also helps to make more efficient use of planting spaces and

Hanging baskets can support many different plants and are a good way of extending the garden upwards.

SLOW-GROWING PLANTS

The following cultivars of popular garden plants are relatively slow-growing and are therefore suitable to small gardens:

Buddleia davidii 'Nanho Purple' (butterfly bush)
Purple-red flowers, height 1.5m (5ft), spread 1.2m (4ft)

Choisya ternata 'Sundance' (Mexican orange blossom)
Evergreen, golden foliage, height and spread 1.2m (4ft)

Escallonia 'Red Elf'
Semi-evergreen, red flowers, height and spread 1.2m (4ft)

Forsythia suspensa
Quite vigorous but, unlike most others, it can be trained along wires against a wall or fence. Height and spread 2.4m (8ft)

Lavandula augustifolia 'Hidcote'
Purple-blue flowers. Height 45cm (18in), spread 30cm (1ft)

Magnolia stellata
Slowly reaches a height and spread of 1.2m (4ft)

Philadelphus 'Manteau d'Hermine' (mock orange blossom)
Fragrant white flowers. Height and spread 1.2m (4ft)

Pleioblastus auricomus
Golden variegated bamboo, growing to a height of 1.2m (4ft) and with a spread of 60cm (2ft)

Potentilla fruticosa 'Red Ace'
Orange flowers. Height 45cm (18in), spread 90cm (3ft)

Rosmarinus officinalis 'Miss Jessopp's Upright'
A compact, upright rosemary. Height 1.5m (5ft), spread 90cm (3ft)

Potentilla fruticosa 'Red Ace'

Santolina chamaecyparis-susnana (cotton lavender)
A compact variety, height and spread 45cm (18in)

Note: the specific name **nana** *usually indicates that a plant is relatively compact and slow-growing.*

produces a more attractive and interesting route round the garden. These paths are made up of both square and rectangular paving slabs, making it easier to lay complex patterns around the planted areas. The slabs have been laid directly onto soil so that, should more space be needed for planting, some can be taken up or moved at will.

A place to relax

The summer house provides a sheltered place to sit and admire the beautiful views over the neighbouring fields and hills. In order to fulfil the need for a greenhouse, the solid roof has been replaced with a plastic one so that seedlings can be raised in here during the spring. A glass roof would have been equally appropriate. The new garden room also provides warmth and shelter with views across the garden, and the opportunity to grow some indoor or tender plants. The design incorporates a garden bench seat on a tiny paved and gravelled area beside a pool that has a view through a 'rustic' arch to some planting beyond.

Water features

The pool itself is a fibreglass mould put in at ground level so it is integrated as naturally as possible with the bog planting. Both pool and bog garden are surrounded by gravel and crazy paving, since both materials fit easily around the complicated shapes of the water features. The area of gravel is edged with pieces of stone to prevent it from mixing with the border soil, and the crazy paving has been only partially pointed to allow carpeting plants and miniature bulbs to be grown inbetween some of the stones.

Supports for climbing plants

The original garden contained a number of well-established climbers which had to be incorporated into the new design, but the owner wants to introduce some more. Apart from the summer house and parts of the fences, there was nowhere for them to grow before, so the new design includes a 'rustic' arch and a small pergola. The arch, together with some fairly tall planting, has helped to create a small secret corner, with a curved stepping-stone path providing a walk through from the pond to the five-bar gate. The pergola, though not large, is positioned so that, when it is fully clothed with climbing plants, it will cast an area of shade on the patio outside the garden room on hot sunny days.

Even with the 'rustic arch', the pergola and the summer house, the garden felt rather open and featureless, so some 'rustic' poles have been set into the ground on either side of the arch to enhance the feeling of secrecy, with further poles placed behind the seat to make it a little more secluded.

A place for alpines

The new garden design includes a scree bed to house a prized collection of alpine plants, and perhaps some alpine bulbs, which prefer to grow in rock crevices and beds of stone rather than in soil. Most alpines are quite small and therefore ideal for a small scree bed like this one. There are many other tiny alpines which, though not strictly scree-loving, will also be happy in the scree bed.

This feature consists of a low, raised bed made of dry stone and filled with broken rock and gravel laid to a depth of about 10cm (4in) over light, well drained, weed-free topsoil, chosen with a relatively high pH, because many scree plants prefer alkaline soil. A few larger pieces of rock, including some tufa, have been added to provide extra height and character.

Hanging space

There are a number of places on the pergola, the rear wall of the house and part of the summer house where hanging baskets can be displayed. These provide more planting space and present the ideal opportunity to experiment with a series of seasonal displays. For more variety, a large wooden tub has been suspended by strong chains from a tripod of heavy 'rustic' poles, just like a giant hanging basket, and this has been filled with tomatoes, strawberries, lettuce, radish and herbs. The whole structure stands about 1.8m (6ft) high, with the tub about 45cm (18in) off the ground, so there is plenty of room to grow other plants underneath. This two-tier style of planting is especially useful in small gardens.

Lighting

For the finishing touches, soft, low-level lights have been installed around the pool and patio area so that, even if the weather is not warm enough for sitting outside, these two areas can be appreciated from inside the house at night. A couple of spotlights have also been fixed onto the pergola, and a hidden light has been placed in a shrub just beyond the arch in the secret corner.

ALPINES SUITABLE FOR A SMALL SCREE BED

Acinos corsicus
Grey hummocks and tiny pink flowers

Androsace primuloides
Neat woolly rosettes of leaves form a mat which bears clear pink flowers

Antennaria parvifolia
(cat's ears)
Silvery evergreen mat with white flowers

Artemisia schmidtiana 'Nana' (wormwood)
Bright silver, feathery mats

Helianthemum (rock rose)
Silver-grey foliage, flowers in a range of colours

Helichrysum orientale
Mats of silver foliage and yellow flowers

Helianthemum nummularium

Hypericum coris
Yellow flowers for many weeks

Leontopodium alpinum
(edelweiss)
Grey foliage and white flowers

Potentilla megalantha
(and others)
Grey foliage, yellow flowers

Raoulia hookeri
Tight mats of tiny silver-grey leaves

White *Helianthemum*

Sagina subulata 'Aurea' (sandwort)
Low hummocks of golden foliage

Saxifraga paniculata
Various, all producing attractive tight rosettes of foliage and flowers of various colours

Sempervivum (houseleek)
There are many different types of suitable houseleek

Teucrium polium
Silver-grey foliage and yellow flowers

Thymus (thyme)
A wide selection of mat-forming types, often with coloured foliage., mainly pink or mauve flowers.

Vitaliana primuliflora
Tight green hummocks with stemless yellow flowers

Thymus

Functional front garden

Dimensions – This garden is about 7.2m (24ft) wide and 3.6m (12ft) deep

Aspect – The garden faces east, with the mid-day sun shining in from the left. The right-hand end of the bungalow is, therefore, in shade

Soil type – The soil is light with a neutral pH

Other information – The garden is wrapped around two sides of a bungalow on the corner of a quiet street. It is, in effect, a front and side garden with a driveway as the only access to the front door and a low wall all round the outside. The front door is connected with the driveway by a concrete path about 30cm (12in) out from the wall of the house. The path continues across the front and round the side of the bungalow to a side gate in a fence leading to the back garden. The existing lawn is 'L'-shaped with a narrow border round most of the edge

Garden plan

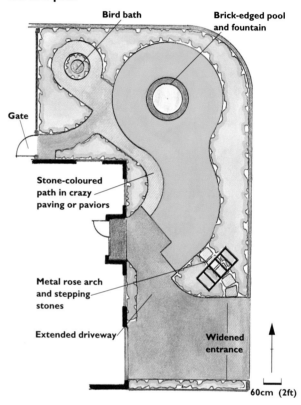

This lay-out provides good access to the front door and an attractive garden that stretches all round the corner of the house and still has room to incorporate a water feature, stepping stones and a bird bath.

The brief

The driveway and its entrance were too tight and needed widening to allow easier car parking and manoeuvering; the route to the front door was also too narrow and needed some widening along with the area immediately in front of the door itself. The lay-out was boring and needed to be more imaginative and appealing, especially as the garden is on a prominent corner of the street. Low maintenance is not a priority – the owners were keen to develop a first-class lawn, but wanted a garden which was not too fussy or complicated to look after.

Practicalities

The driveway and access to the front door were most urgently in need of being redesigned in a way that would make it easier to park the car and walk to the front door without being tempted to cross the garden. The new lay-out has had to provide enough space for several people to use the front door at the same time and to make it easier to take shopping from the car into the house without disturbing the plants or lawn.

The first thing to have been changed is the width of the entrance off the road. The brick wall and its pillar have been moved back by about 60cm (2ft) to improve access and make it easier to drive in at an angle without catching the side of the car on the pillar or fence post. The possibility of also widening the dropped kerb along the roadside was considered but could have meant lengthy consultations with the local council, and would probably have been quite expensive to do. The moving of the pillar and the wall back meant that a larger section of wall had to be demolished and a small piece of pavement disturbed to make room for a foundation for the new pillar.

An imaginative yet functional front garden

THE NEW DESIGN

A new surface

The wider entrance has obviously made it possible to extend the driveway but also to take part of it across towards the front door in the form of a generous path. It was tempting to keep down costs by paving this extra area in a completely separate material and not disturb the existing driveway and its black tarmac. The overriding priority, however, was to improve access and to make the whole area more spacious, so the same surface has been used all over. This meant chipping away the surface of the existing tarmac, taking out some soil from those areas which had previously been garden and replacing it with well-consolidated hardcore and a layer of scalpings on top. A stock brick kerb was then put around the edges in a way that allowed the new surface to end up flush with it. It was decided to use red-brown tarmac over the whole area right up to the front porch, so a base course of tarmac was rolled down on top of the scalpings, then a thin layer of red wearing course put right over the top of both the old and the new area to produce a much more useful and spacious entrance and car parking area.

A winding path

The next job has been to put a new winding path, together with a small area of paving, round and towards the back gate. This has meant breaking up the old concrete paths, making arrangements for an electricity supply to the water feature and recycling the resulting concrete hardcore as a base for the new path. Stone-coloured block paviors have been used with a

Planting against the house ensures that the garden will look attractive both from the road and from within.

block pavior edging which has first been concreted on to the hardcore base. Scalpings have been used in a layer on top of the hardcore, followed by a layer of sand on which the block paviors have been vibrated down so that they end up flush with the edges. Quite a lot of the blocks had to be cut to fit round the various curves but the end result is very neat and satisfactory. The wooden gate has been replaced by a more attractive wrought-iron one with a steel hoop over the top to provide support for a climbing plant.

The path to the front door can be made more attractive with planting down either side.

The water feature

The next job was to construct the pool which has been built around a circular moulded pool purchased from a local garden centre. It has a diameter of 1.2m (4ft) and a depth of 60cm (2ft) and was set into the ground at a depth which enabled the 45cm (18in) wide brick edging to be laid flush with the lawn. A plastic over-flow has been plumbed in (using standard domestic fittings) and runs into a small soakaway.

A groove was made in the top edge of the plastic for the submersible pump cable and a small under-ground chamber has been built beneath part of the brick edging for a water-tight connection to the mains electricity supply. This chamber has been linked up to the soakaway so that it cannot flood, but the soil is light and well drained so this should not be a prob-lem. It would not be such a satisfactory arrangement in poorly drained, clay soil.

Focal points

The metal rose arch has been included more as a focal point than as a useful feature. It does have a small step-ping stone path going from the driveway to the lawn but this is only likely to be used for maintaining the border. It has, however, provided somewhere to grow a climbing rose and created just a little privacy at one point. The stone bird table, which has been set in to the circular bed at the side of the bungalow is another attractive focal point and is close enough to the win-dow to be watched from indoors.

The lawn

The owners of the bungalow have always wanted a really top-quality lawn and felt that here was the ideal opportunity and location for one. Although the cheapest (and sometimes the best) way to produce a good lawn is to sow the very finest grass seed on an exceptionally well-prepared seedbed, a quicker solution would be to use sea-washed turf instead. This contains many fine grasses but will be much harder to look after than a lawn containing more robust grass species. The fungal disease *Fusarium* could become a serious problem particularly during the spring and autumn.

Preparing the borders

Only a few plants have been retained. These included plants in the narrow border to the left of the driveway, a *Cotoneaster horizontalis* beneath the window next to the garage, a clematis on the corner of the bungalow and a few fairly mature shrubs against the fence at the side of the bungalow and a short distance along the boundary wall. Everywhere else was stripped bare and dug over to a depth of about 45cm (18in), with plenty of well-rotted manure worked in. This help to store moisture in the light soil. Before planting, the borders were lightly compacted and levelled off to just above the height of the lawn.

Planting and colour co-ordination

Both the garage and the front door used to be bright blue but since they were due to be re-painted it was decided to change their colour to one more sympa-thetic to the garden. The same applied to the two short lengths of fencing which had, originally, been stained 'red cedar'. The colours most compatible with flowers and foliage are olive-green or a yellowish-green (as opposed to a blue-green) or even khaki. Among the browns, the most appropriate are the chocolate browns, rather than the reddish or bright yellow-browns. The doors have now been re-painted yellow, and the fences a soft chocolate brown. In addition, the original black guttering and down pipes have been changed to brown, giving the bungalow a more mellow appearance.

Gravel paths are relatively inexpensive and can act as a useful burglar deterrent.

The two trees outside the garden obviously influence whatever is growing directly beneath them, which is one reason why the mature shrubs next to the side fence have been left alone. It would take quite a long time to re-establish the same degree of cover with new plants in this position. Much of the planting round the outside edge of the garden is herbaceous with plenty of summer flowers but a few evergreens

More could be made of this front entrance by using a larger number of plants and adding paving outside the front door.

for winter interest. No attempt has been made to screen off the garden with tall plants because it has been designed to look attractive from the road as well as from within, but one or two taller items have been included to provide some variation in height.

A collection of plant boxes and pots can bring plants to an area which has permanent concrete.

CLIMBING PLANTS

Climbers used against a house can help to soften the look of the walls, especially in a front garden where the house will be seen from the road. The planting must not, however, interfere with the inspection of external electricity and gas meters or with cleaning the windows.

Clematis
Twining climbers and herbaceous perennials producing masses of flowers in a wide range of colours. Climbers best against walls or trellis. Prefers roots in shade and shoots in sun

Hedera (ivy)
Evergreen trailing perennials and self-clinging climbers which tolerate a wide range of conditions, including shade. Growth is rapid once plants are well established. Many varieties available with range of leaf shape and variegations

Pyracantha
Evergreen, spiny, summer-flowering shrub. Needs a sheltered site in sun or partial shade and fertile soil. Berries produced in autumn and winter

Parthenocissus (Virginia creeper)
Vigorous, partly self-clinging climbers with attractive, vine-like leaves and excellent autumn colour

Wisteria sinensis
Woody-stemmed, twining climber producing spectacular racemes of flowers in early summer. Best in sun and fertile, well-drained soil. Requires pruning after flowering and in winter

Garden construction

In many cases, garden construction is quite straightforward and can be tackled by almost anyone. The methods are described in the following pages.

Lawns

Preparing the site

Before sowing seed or laying turf, clear the site of perennial weeds and grasses by digging them out or killing them off. Next, dig or rotovate the ground and then level it. To do this, rake it approximately level then simply tread the surface in a systematic way, moving up and down the site, placing all your weight on your heels. Do not roll the ground.

Once the ground is level, clear the site of any large stones then rake and tread it once more, removing any stones you turn up in the process. Continue doing this until you have a flat, smooth surface.

Sowing seed

Sowing grass seed is best done during the spring when the warmer weather has begun to heat up the soil and the chances of rain are good. Evenly scatter the seed at a rate of about 20g (a small fistful) per square metre (⅔oz per yd) onto the prepared surface, then lightly rake it in. If the soil is dusty, gently roll the seed into the surface.

Once the lawn is established, keep feeding and weeding as separate operations rather than using a combined product which may damage the grass (see Seasonal Maintenance chart, opposite).

TURF OR SEED?

Turf	Seed
Instant results	Relatively slow
Can be laid at almost any time of the year, except during frost and drought	Best sown in spring
Limited choice in grass type	A wide range of grass types available
More expensive than seed	May require a little more preparation than turf and, initially, weeds may be more of a problem

Edging a seeded lawn

Prepare a seed bed a little larger than planned and sow seed about 30cm (12in) beyond the required limits. Once the lawn has begun to establish itself, cut it to shape and either kill off or dig in the unwanted grass, or move it to another part of the garden (where it is within easy reach of the mower) and grow it as a small nursery area for future patching.

Alternatively, edge the site with turves, which is a good method to use in conjunction with timber edging. Before sowing any seed, set one row of turves all around the edge of the site so that they are flush with the surface of the seed bed. This will eventually produce a turfed edge about 30cm (12in) wide around the seeded lawn. The disadvantage of this technique, however, is that the turfed edge will always appear slightly different to the seeded areas.

The problem of weeds

Weeds are more of a problem in newly sown rather than turfed lawns because the young grass is less able to cope with such competition. To reduce the problem

HEIGHT AND FREQUENCY OF CUT

This chart indicates the height and frequency to which different quality lawns should be cut for the period late spring to early autumn. The figures given are only a rough guide, and should be varied according to the weather and the state of the turf. Outside the period the height of cut should be increased by 7.5mm (¼in).

Type of lawn

cm	Average	Utility	Paddock
4			
3.5			
3			
2.5			
2			
1.5			
1			
0.5			
0			
	3-5 days	7 days	7 days

CREATING A LAWN BENEATH LARGE TREES

It is better and easier to create a lawn under a deciduous tree which has a light canopy than beneath a tree with dense foliage, such as a large conifer. Initially, turf will produce the best results under any type of tree but, in the long term, the success of the lawn will depend largely on how you maintain it. Although special shade mixtures of grass seed are available, they tend to produce rather thin growth that is unsuitable for a close-cut lawn and are better used to make areas of semi-wild grass which you can plant up with naturalized bulbs. Ideally, both turfing and seeding should be carried out during spring or early summer, before the leaves of the trees open, otherwise the grass will almost certainly suffer from lack of rain or too little light. In subsequent years, this is also the best time to give the lawn its annual feed of high nitrogen compound fertilizer.

Laying turf

1. Working off a plank and progressing forwards, lay the turves in a bonded fashion, like bricks in a wall. Fit them together as tightly as possible.

2. Once you have laid the turves, work handfuls of fine soil or compost into the joints so that it will encourage the turves to knit together should they shrink a little.

Edging

A brick edging is especially useful where a driveway or patio abuts a lawn. The bricks should be laid on a concrete foundation a little wider than the bricks and about 7.5cm (3in) deep.

Timber edging, made from pressure-treated soft wood, provides a very precise, long-lasting edge. Saw cuts in the wood every 5cm (2in) to make it easier to bend it around the curves of the lawn area.

of weeds growing through a newly sown lawn, leave the prepared seedbed for a few weeks before sowing. During this time, a new flush of weeds will start to grow, which you can either uproot with a hoe or kill with a herbicide, such as glyphosate, that will not poison or taint the soil. After sowing the seed, a handful of weeds may well germinate with the grass, but most of these should die out once regular mowing starts.

If weeds are a persistent problem once the lawn has started to grow, wait at least eight months before contemplating the use of a selective herbicide. You may then only need to spot-treat relatively few weeds rather than spray the whole area.

The problem of stones

If you are trying to establish a seeded lawn on very stony ground, you may well find that, despite having thoroughly cleared the site in the first place, small stones keep appearing on the surface of the ground. To deal with this, wait until the new grass has established itself and needs its first cut before carefully raking the stones off with a wire or rigid plastic leaf rake. This will not damage the new grass and the established grass roots should stop more stones from surfacing.

Mowing regime

For a seeded lawn, wait until the grass has reached a height of about 2.5cm (1in) before mowing. For a turf lawn, you may need to cut it soon after laying if it is

vigorous, but, ideally, wait until it is difficult to pull up the individual turves.

In all cases, use a rotary mower for the first few cuts as it is less likely to dislodge or rip up the new grass than a cylinder mower. In general, rotary mowers are better for slightly uneven lawns as they will not scalp higher areas to the same extent as cylinder mowers.

SEASONAL MAINTENANCE

Early spring Scarify and cut if not frosty. Apply a high nitrogen spring feed as weather turns milder and water in immediately afterwards. Mow as often as necessary.

Late spring Continue to mow regularly. Apply one more dose of spring feed 6–7 weeks after the first and water in. Treat lawn weeds with a selective herbicide – follow the instructions very carefully. Scarify if not already done.

Summer Continue to mow as often as necessary. Irrigate if very dry. Apply one more high nitrogen feed about 8 weeks after the last one if the soil is poor and sandy. Continue to spot-treat weeds but avoid large scale use of herbicide, especially in drought.

Early autumn Continue to mow as necessary. Keep fallen leaves raked up. Apply a high potash/phosphate autumn feed and water in but no sooner than 6 weeks after the previous feed. Continue to spot treat weeds.

Late autumn Keep fallen leaves raked up. Apply insecticide against wireworms and leatherjackets if necessary. Mow as necessary, but not in frosty weather. Scarify if moss is very bad, otherwise wait until spring.

Winter No activity except leaf clearing and, if necessary, mowing in mild spells.

Note: *It may be necessary to use a fungicide against fusarium and other diseases, more particularly in spring and autumn. The use of moss killer is of doubtful value and not recommended.*

Patios and paving

Choice of materials

There is an ever increasing range of materials available for hard surfacing and your choice will depend partly upon what you can afford and partly upon practical considerations. For example, areas of paving with curved edges cannot easily be surfaced with large, square or rectangular slabs; in such a case smaller units like bricks, setts or block paviors would be more suitable because they are easier to cut to a curve.

Foundations for patios and paving

Areas of paving are only as stable as the ground (or foundations) on which they are built. Clay can cause problems by constantly shrinking and expanding, whereas hard stony ground is usually the most stable. The nature and thickness of any foundation will, therefore, have to depend on the underlying soil and on the use of the paving.

The depth of foundations

A driveway built on clay soil will need a much deeper foundation – possibly 22.5cm (9in) thick – than a patio on stony ground – perhaps only 7.5cm (3in)

Filling in beneath a raised patio

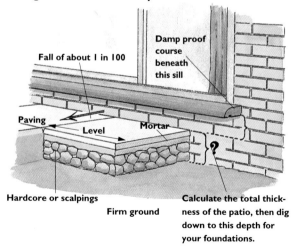

This shows how to calculate how far below the damp course patio construction should start.

Using pegs to mark out a rectangular raised patio

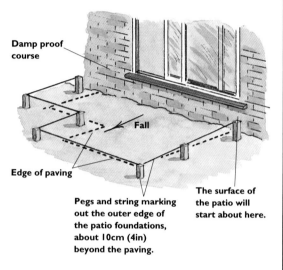

Pegs should go deep enough into the ground so that they remain firm even after the soil has been excavated. They can then be used to guide levels.

Using pegs to mark out a curved raised patio

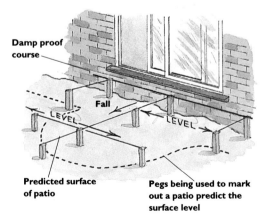

The centre row of level pegs must extend to the apex of the curve. Levels for all the others can then be set from this line.

MATERIALS COMMONLY USED AS A FOUNDATION

Hardcore (bricks or concrete broken into small pieces): This is relatively inexpensive material and can be used to fill large spaces quite cheaply, but is unsuitable directly beneath a layer of sand because the sand will filter down in between the pieces.

Scalpings: (small pieces of crushed rock and dust) This is more expensive than hardcore but will compact to produce a thinner, denser foundation. It is often used over the top of hardcore.

thick. Calculate how thick your foundation should be, add the thickness of your chosen paving and about 1.5cm (½in) for the thickness of mortar on to which the paving is to be laid. This will give the total thickness of the whole construction and enable you to judge how much soil to excavate. Where paving abuts a building, its surface must be at least 15cm (6in) below the damp proof course.

A 'fall'

All paving must have a 'fall' or slope so that water will run off. Paving against a house will usually be laid with a fall of 1:100 (that is, 1cm per metre or about 1in per 3yd) away from the house, but will be level across, in line with the brickwork.

Digging a foundation for paving at or slightly below ground level

Dig the soil so that the floor of the excavation is at the correct depth, has the appropriate 'fall' and is about 10cm (4in) larger all round than the area of paving. If the paving is likely to end up significantly below ground level, dig out an extra strip about 7.5cm (3in) deep for a wall foundation around those sides most likely to need one. The width of this strip foundation should be twice as wide as the wall you intend to build. You should also incorporate some form of drainage along these walls, since water is likely to build up in these low parts of the patio.

Placing the foundations

Spread the hardcore or scalpings out evenly over the surface and compact with a vibrating plate until they are at exactly the right level in relation to the surrounding area and have the correct 'fall'. If a wall foundation has been dug out you can either lay concrete in the base or fill it with hardcore or scalpings.

Materials	Advantages	Disadvantages
Slabs with a patterned or stone effect surface (moulded)	Can produce some interesting effects. Relatively inexpensive. Quite easy to lay.	Not very strong. Not easy to cut to a curve. May have a very uneven surface. Not good for vehicular use unless on a very strong foundation.
Smooth slabs (hydraulically pressed)	Usually have a smooth or textured surface. Thicker and stronger than moulded slabs. Strong enough for vehicular use.	Heavier than moulded slabs. Comparatively expensive. Difficult to cut, especially to a curve.
Concrete block and brick paviors, setts etc	Can be used to create interesting patterns and effects. Easy to handle. Most are suitable for vehicular use. Not particularly difficult to cut (with a disc cutter) and lay to a curve. No pointing required in joints.	Often expensive. Some types can be awkward to lay. Tend to appear too modern against old buildings.
Stock bricks (hard enough to use for paving)	Produce an attractive rustic appearance. Often suitable in conjunction with older buildings. Can be cut and laid to a curve. Suitable for vehicular use.	Expensive. Not always easy to lay. Usually need pointing.
Natural stone	Attractive 'natural' effect.	Expensive. Can be difficult to cut to a curve. (Crazy paving does not, of course, need cutting.) May become slippery in winter. Most needs pointing (especially crazy paving).

A comparison of the different types of paving materials.

A sequence for laying slabs

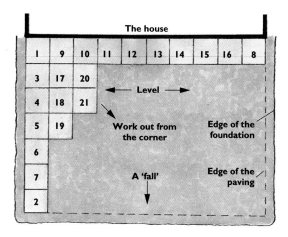

Follow this sequence as a guide for using the levels of the slabs you have just laid to guide the levels of the next batch of slabs.

Laying slabs

The most usual and often the easiest way to lay slabs is on top of blobs of wet mortar. Lay your first slab at one of the high corners of the foundation, setting it to an appropriate fall in one direction and level in the other. Lay a second slab in the corresponding lowest corner, again to a 'fall' but level across. Now stretch a string tightly between the two so that it lines up exactly with their outer edges and follows the 'fall' from the top to the bottom. Lay the rest of the slabs in the row using the string to guide you and a spirit level to ensure that the slabs are level across. Once the first row is complete you can lay a second row of slabs along the top edge, each matching the downwards slope of the one next to it but level across. You will be able to build outwards using the levels of your previous slabs as a reference.

For slabs over about 30cm (12in) square, use five blobs of mortar so that, once a slab has been gently tapped down to the right level with the handle of a club hammer, the blobs join to form, more or less, a complete bed of mortar.

Laying small slabs, blocks or bricks

Follow the same process as before but lay the edges all the way round. Then take a long straight piece of wood and rest it on two edges across a corner.

Working out from the corner, set an area of paving on a rough bed rather than on blobs of mortar and tap the units down until each one just fits beneath the piece of wood.

A raised patio

For this, you will need a series of supporting walls built on top of concrete 'strip' foundations. These

---

Brick work

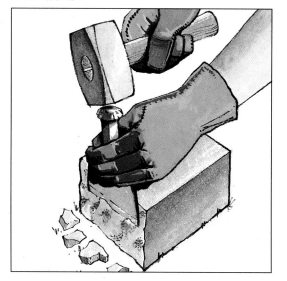

1. You can cut most bricks and block paviors by placing them on a firm, level surface and using a club hammer and bolster.

2. On a small scale you can compact bricks or block paviors into a sand bed using a club hammer and stout piece of timber.

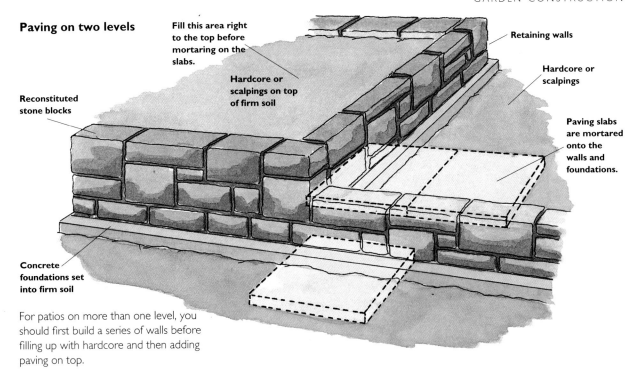

Paving on two levels

Fill this area right to the top before mortaring on the slabs.

Hardcore or scalpings on top of firm soil

Retaining walls

Hardcore or scalpings

Reconstituted stone blocks

Paving slabs are mortared onto the walls and foundations.

Concrete foundations set into firm soil

For patios on more than one level, you should first build a series of walls before filling up with hardcore and then adding paving on top.

foundations are normally put in perfectly level, perhaps to a thickness of 7.5–15cm (3–6in) depending on ground conditions, and twice the width of the walls. Although these walls will, initially, be constructed level, some will have to end up with a slope or taper so that a 'fall' can be introduced in the paving laid over the top. For a stone wall you can quite easily vary the thickness of the top course from one end to the other but if the wall is brick you will need to cut some wedges.

Once the walls have set properly, you will be able to fill carefully and compact inside with hardcore or scalpings right to the top. You can then lay the paving as described earlier but with an overhang of about 1.5cm (½in) all round. Pegs and string can be very useful in predicting where the surface (and the foundations) of a patio, whether raised or not, will end up in relation to the surrounding area. This in turn will help you to decide on the height of walls or the depth of foundations.

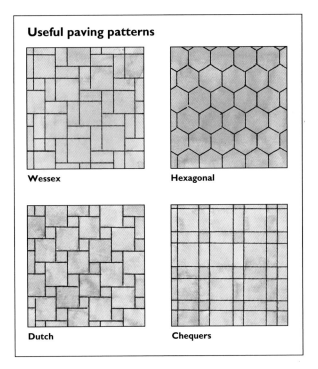

Useful paving patterns

Wessex

Hexagonal

Dutch

Chequers

MORTAR MIXES

For the mortar bed: 1 part of cement + 8 parts of sharp sand

For pointing: 1 part cement + 6 parts of sharp sand

The mix for pointing must be carefully measured out each time (batched) so that it turns out exactly the same colour throughout the job.

Pointing

If your paving has joints which need pointing, wait until the paving has set quite firm on its mortar base. Work off planks or boards and use a pointing trowel to feed a moist mortar mix into the joints. Remember to batch the pointing mix (see Mortar Mixes, left).

Paths

If anything, an even wider range of materials is used for paths than for patios. Below is a list of materials which can be added to those already described under Patios and Paving.

Drainage

Always ensure that whatever material you use for path construction, its surface can drain efficiently. This might mean incorporating a slight cross-fall or crown so that water drains to the edge. In many cases it would then flow into a planted border but if your path is to have an edging, gaps can be left to allow water through. The only exception is for paths laid directly on to soil, such as bark chippings.

Foundations

The average thickness for a path foundation is about 10cm (4in) depending on what the path is used for, the type of surface and the ground conditions. Scalpings are the most common material, but you could use hardcore as an economical alternative for deeper foundations in soft ground, possibly topped with scalpings. In most cases you place the foundation materials after the edgings have been installed but brick or block edging may sometimes go in on top of the foundation material. It is important to know how deep the foundation material should be to allow room for the other materials on top.

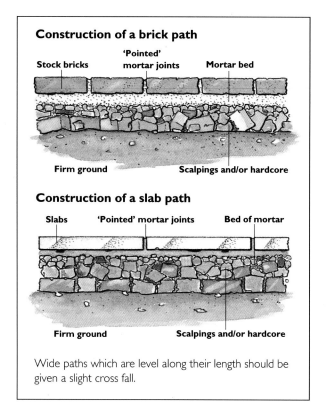

Construction of a brick path

Stock bricks · 'Pointed' mortar joints · Mortar bed

Firm ground · Scalpings and/or hardcore

Construction of a slab path

Slabs · 'Pointed' mortar joints · Bed of mortar

Firm ground · Scalpings and/or hardcore

Wide paths which are level along their length should be given a slight cross fall.

To calculate this, decide whether or not the surface of your path should be flush with the top of the edging. Gravel or shingle, for example, would usually end up about 2cm (¾in) below the edging. Add to this the thickness of the gravel itself, about 2cm (¾in) and then the thickness of the actual foundation materials. In this example the base would be about 5cm (2in) of compacted hoggin on top of 7.5cm (3in) of scalpings. This would mean that the surface of the scalpings should be 9cm (about 3½in) below the top of the edging, so the path would have to be dug down a further 7.5cm (3in) to make room for scalpings.

Material	Advantages	Disadvantages	The type of edging	Other comments
Gravels and shingle	Inexpensive and easy to lay	Can kick onto a lawn, be picked up by young children and can carry indoors on shoes	Timber, bricks or blocks, rope tiles, or concrete kerbs	May need topping up or replacing after a year or two
Self-binding gravels	Attractive, hard wearing and much less mobile than gravel or shingle	Expensive and relatively difficult to lay	As above	Must have a well-drained surface, with a fall or crown
Bark chippings	Ideal in a woodland setting, easy to put down and need only compacted soil beneath. Relatively inexpensive	Can kick onto a lawn. May tread indoors as a brown stain in wet weather	Log or sawn timber	In time they will need topping up or replacing

A comparison of different path construction materials.

Laying a concrete path

1. Set out two stout timber edges either level or with a slight cross-fall and so that the surface of your path finishes at, or just below, ground level.

2. Remove any soft soil and build up to within about 7.5cm (3in) of the top with well-rammed hardcore.

3. Pour in and rake out concrete, which should be stiff rather than runny, overfilling the space a little.

4. Tamp the concrete down to the timber edges with a piece of wood, adding more concrete as necessary. Cover over with a sheet of polythene and leave the concrete to 'cure'. To achieve an exposed aggregate (pebbly) finish, remove the polythene after about five hours and *gently* wash and brush the surface to expose, but not loosen, the top layer of stones. Replace the polythene and allow the path to cure completely.

PATH SURFACING MATERIALS

Gravel

This consists of small, angular pieces of crushed stone or rock, perhaps 1cm (⅜in) across and mostly brown, red, grey or white. It is spread no deeper than about 2cm (¾in) over a hard base, like hoggin.

Shingle

Similar to gravel but rounded, washed stones usually a golden-greyish brown and laid to the same depth.

Self-binding path gravels

Most of these are a reddish-brown or grey. Spread over a hoggin or scalpings base to a depth of about 4cm (1½in) and compacted with a vibrating plate or roller they produce a hard, smooth, gritty but attractive surface (which must have efficient drainage).

Bricks and block paviors

Normally used with brick or block edging, these can be laid on mortar as described under Patios and Paving or, alternatively, compacted down onto a bed of damp, sharp sand about 4cm (1½in) thick, overlying compacted scalpings or hoggin. The sand is raked out between the edgings then an area of paviors set on top so that they stick up above the edging by about 1.5cm (½in). As paviors are designed to create patterns with no need for pointing, they must be packed in tightly, with pieces cut to fit as necessary. Once a metre (or a yard) or so has been set out, the paviors can be banged down using a stout piece of wood and a club hammer until they are flush with the edges. A vibrating plate can also be used for this, but if the blocks go down too far, a slightly thicker layer of sand should be used underneath. This technique is not appropriate for bricks which need joints and pointing.

Note: If hoggin is not available as a base, you might be tempted to use scalpings. The disadvantage of this is that, in time, pieces of the scalpings (which look totally different from gravel or shingle) kick out and mix in. It is sometimes possible to prevent or delay this by mixing a generous amount of cement dust into the surface of the scalpings before compacting them.

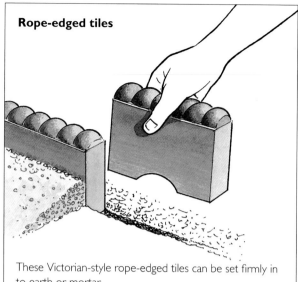

Rope-edged tiles

These Victorian-style rope-edged tiles can be set firmly in to earth or mortar.

Types of edging

You will need to edge any loose path materials to prevent them spreading, but you may wish to add edging to more stable materials purely for aesthetic reasons. In most cases, you would install the edges before building the rest of the path but in the case of brick or block edging there might be some benefit in putting down some of the general foundation materials first and setting the edging on top.

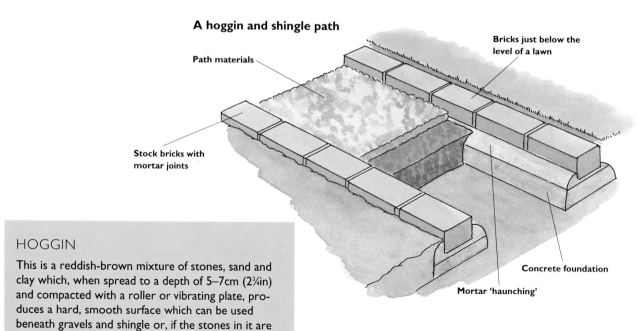

A hoggin and shingle path

Path materials

Bricks just below the level of a lawn

Stock bricks with mortar joints

Concrete foundation

Mortar 'haunching'

HOGGIN

This is a reddish-brown mixture of stones, sand and clay which, when spread to a depth of 5–7cm (2¾in) and compacted with a roller or vibrating plate, produces a hard, smooth surface which can be used beneath gravels and shingle or, if the stones in it are not too large, as a surface in its own right.

Depth of construction of this type of path will vary according to soil conditions.

Brick or block pavior edging

This should be set on a small 'strip' concrete foundation at least 15cm (6in) wide and about 7.5cm (3in) deep (more in soft ground). Mark out both edges of the path and dig out a narrow foundation trench to the appropriate depth. In cases where the ground is very soft, and the path needs a deeper than average foundation of hardcore or scalpings, dig out the whole area, including the edges, spread and compact some of the hardcore or scalpings then concrete your edges on top of this. Whichever approach you adopt, it is most important to ensure that the top surface of your edging blocks ends up at the correct level in relation to both the surface of the path and to the surrounding area.

The edging blocks will be set onto the 'strip' foundation using mortar. They will also have mortar between them (like bricks in a wall) and a generous 'haunching' of mortar on the outside for extra stability. You will find a string line or a long straight piece of wood useful to help create a smooth level down each side of the path.

Timber edging

Use strips of pressure-treated timber about 10cm (4in) wide and 2cm (¾in) thick for the edges and timber 3.8 x 3.8cm (1½in square) for supporting pegs. Start by marking out the whole path and excavating the soil to a depth of about 10cm (4in), depending upon the type of construction you are planning. Firmly bang in pegs about 30–35cm (12–14in) long, every 90cm (3ft) or so down either side of the path, making sure the tops strike a smooth level that follows the contours of the ground. When the edging has been nailed on, flush with the tops, the pegs should end up on the outside.

If you need to bend the edging strips, make saw cuts halfway through the wood about every 5cm (2in) on what will be the inside of the curve, so that when the bend is made the saw cuts close up. It is wise to paint extra wood preservative into these or any other saw cuts. You may need extra pegs around steep curves and some on the inside as well as on the outside of the edging. Once all the edging is in place you can fill the centre with your path materials.

Types of edging

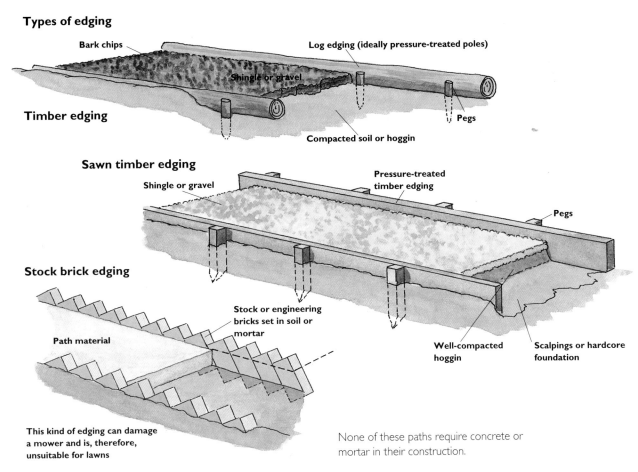

Bark chips
Log edging (ideally pressure-treated poles)
Shingle or gravel
Timber edging
Pegs
Compacted soil or hoggin

Sawn timber edging
Shingle or gravel
Pressure-treated timber edging
Pegs

Stock brick edging
Stock or engineering bricks set in soil or mortar
Path material
Well-compacted hoggin
Scalpings or hardcore foundation

This kind of edging can damage a mower and is, therefore, unsuitable for lawns

None of these paths require concrete or mortar in their construction.

Steps

Taking measurements

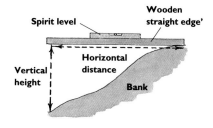

Spirit level

Wooden straight edge'

Vertical height

Horizontal distance

Bank

Steps up a bank

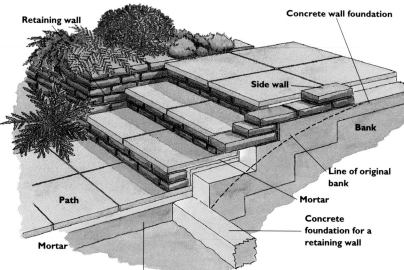

Retaining wall

Concrete wall foundation

Side wall

Bank

Line of original bank

Path

Mortar

Mortar

Concrete foundation for a retaining wall

Scalpings or hardcore

Typical step construction

Tread

Riser

Concrete and/or mortar

Hardcore or scalpings

It is important that all the steps in a flight are exactly the same size, as any variation in the height of the riser or the depth of the tread can lead to accidents.

If you are using retaining in walls in conjunction with steps, put in the wall foundations first. You will then be able to build up the walls first or build them up as you construct the steps.

EXAMPLE

Total height of the bank = 170cm (68in)
Average riser = 15cm (6in)
Number of risers = 170 ÷ 150 = 11 risers with 5cm
Left over (68 ÷ 6 = 11 with 2in left over).
Share these 5cm (2in) between the 11 risers to make each riser 15.4cm (6 ⅛in)
Check: 15.4 x 11 = 169.4cm – only 6mm short and good enough (6 ⅛ x 11 = 67 ⅝in – only ⅛in short)

Calculating the size and number of steps

To calculate the size and number of steps, measure the overall height and distance to be covered. Use a spirit level, a long, straight length of wood and a tape measure. Place one end of the of wood at the top of the bank then, standing at the bottom of the bank at the point where the steps are to start, raise the other end until the spirit level shows it to be horizontal. Measure from the free end of the wood down to the ground to find the height of the bank. To find the distance to be covered, measure along the piece of wood, still held horizontally, from the free end to where it touches the top of the bank.

Then decide on a reasonable height for a riser, in this case 15cm (6in), and calculate how many risers

would fit into the overall height, 170cm(68in) in this measurement. If you are using metric measurements it is easier to work in millimetres for the calculations. If it does not work out exactly but leaves you with millimetres left over, divide these up equally between the whole flight so increasing the height of each riser by just a little. The overall distance back can now be divided by 11 to ascertain the depth of each tread. Now see if you can make a riser of 15.4cm (6⅛in) out of your materials. It will be easy in natural stone but more critical with, say, bricks. If it is impossible to build a riser of that height, take a height you can build and calculate how many you need – again using any spare millimetres in the form of extra mortar.

The building process

If your steps are to travel up a bank, start with a tread but first mark the sides of the flight with string and remove enough soil for your first tread and its foundation. If you can, make your tread go back further than it needs to so that the first riser can use the back section as a foundation. If this is not possible you will have to add some concrete at the back. Tap the front edge of your tread so that it slopes down very slightly for water to drain off.

Before you start to build your first riser on top of this tread, dig out some more soil from the bank to make room for the next tread and the second riser. Set your first riser precisely the correct (calculated) distance back from the front edge of the first tread. Put in the foundation for your next tread behind this riser

and set your tread on it so that it overhangs the riser by approximately 1cm (⅜in).

Make sure that this tread is level and the riser, including the thickness of the tread material, is exactly the correct (calculated) height. Adjust the height of the tread by adding slightly more mortar or by tapping it down all over so that the tread remains level. Once the riser height is correct, tap the front edge of the tread down just a little to create a 'fall' for drainage.

When you position your next riser, on the back of this second tread, measure the distance back from the front face of the previous riser not from the overhanging front edge of the tread. Continue with your flight of steps to the top. If your measurements and calculations were accurate there is a good chance of ending up more or less on target.

Building steps against a wall

1. The sides of the first step (riser) are built right back to meet the wall against which the steps are to be constructed. The structure must be perfectly square and all measurements should be checked carefully.

2. The bottom riser is built up all round and filled with well-compacted concrete or scalpings right back to the wall.

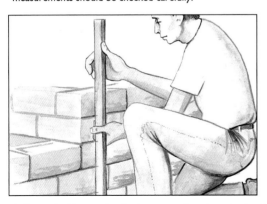

3. As you build upwards, check your work with a spirit level.

4. Subsequent risers are built on top of the first one and filled with scalpings or concrete, leving exactly the right amount of space for each slap to be placed on top. Finally, the slabs are mortared onto each step with a 1cm (⅜in) overhang at the front.

Walls

This section looks at garden walls measuring up to a height of 1.2m (4ft).

Walls can either be 'free standing', used to divide up space in a garden or act as boundaries. They can also be 'retaining', used to hold back a bank or to form a raised bed. All except dry stone walls must have a concrete foundation.

Foundations

You will need to dig a trench which is twice the width of the wall you intend to build, ideally going down 5–7cm (2–3in) into firm subsoil, and perfectly level. This might mean having to dig quite deeply to find firm ground but this is important to get right because, if you were to build a foundation on soft soil, the wall might eventually crack. Take a number of wooden pegs no thicker than 2.5cm (1in) square and knock them into the bottom of the trench to the point where their tops indicate the depth of concrete needed. This will vary with the soil conditions. In clay soil it might be at least 15cm (6in) because of

the problems associated with shrinkage but in hard, stony soil, only about 7.5cm (3in) would be required.

Mix up concrete using 1 part cement plus 6 parts of all-in ballast (and water) and fill up the base of the foundations to the top of each peg. Level off this concrete by tamping it down with a piece of wood, then cover it over with polythene and allow it to cure for a day or two. Never lay concrete in frosty weather unless you incorporate a frost-proofing liquid into the mix.

Building a wall

To lay bricks, blocks or stone, you will need a mortar mix which is creamy but not runny, using 1 part cement, 6 parts soft sand, water and a plasticiser, such as liquid detergent, which is added to make the mortar creamier. Start by setting one brick or block just in from the end or from a corner of the foundations on about 1.5cm (½in) of mortar, and another at the opposite end. Assuming your foundation is level, these two bricks or blocks should be on the same level as each other. Stretch a string tightly between the two bricks, lining it up with the edge furthest away from you. If the distance between the two ends is more than about 2m (6ft 6in) place a temporary brick, on mortar, part of the way along to steady the string. Lay further bricks (or blocks) next to the first so that they too just touch the string. You will, of course, have to 'butter' the end of each new brick with mortar before it is offered up to the one before in order to create a strong vertical joint.

Following the bond of your choice, gradually build up courses on top of one another using the string line to keep your wall straight and a spirit level to check very frequently whether your work is both level and vertical. Bricks can be cut either with a disc cutter or with a club hammer and bolster.

Free-standing brick walls

These can either be constructed as 'half' brick walls, about 10.5cm (4¼in) thick, or as whole brick walls, 21.5cm (8½in) thick. To create a 'half' brick wall you

Laying bricks

1. Start by placing an even bed of mortar along your foundation and set up a string line to guide your first row of bricks.

2. 'Butter' the end of each brick before you place it next to the one already laid. The mortar must be creamy and not too dry, so that it sticks to the brick.

In order to prevent the onset of damp, it is a good idea to lay, just above ground level, two courses of engineering bricks to prevent the upward movement of moisture through the wall. You can also use them along the top as a coping. Most engineering bricks are hard and slightly shiny and are either red, grey or blue-black. They can therefore be used as quite a decorative feature. Corners of 90° are easy to achieve but other angles are likely to create small wedges of brick which will protrude all the way down the corner. You can either trim these off with a disc cutter (taking the precaution of wearing safety goggles) once the wall is complete, or cut the individual bricks to fit during construction.

would lay the bricks using a stretcher bond but for a whole brick wall there are a number of different bonds you could use to lay the bricks. 'Half' brick walls which are lengthy and straight will need piers every 2.4m (8ft) to provide extra stability, and long straight whole brick walls, while not necessarily needing piers, should be constructed with expansion joints every 4m (13ft) or so.

You should always use stock bricks which are especially frost resistant in preference to 'flettons' which are too soft for the exposed conditions in a garden wall. If your foundation has had to go relatively deep underground because of the soil's condition, use concrete blocks to build up to near ground level before changing over to bricks, which will inevitably be more expensive.

A 'free-standing' dry stone wall

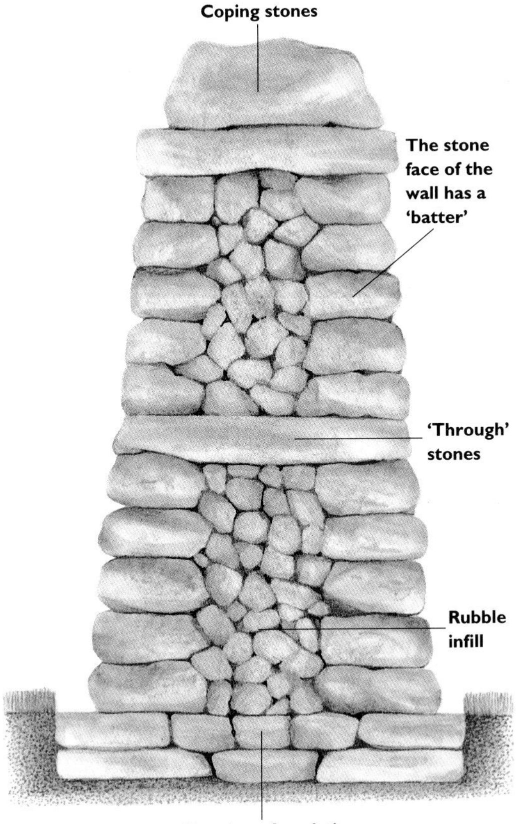

Coping stones

The stone face of the wall has a 'batter'

'Through' stones

Rubble infill

Dry stone foundation set into firm soil

The strength of this wall will depend upon how well stones are fitted together.

English bond

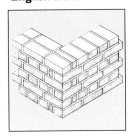

This bond will produce a strong, 'free-standing' wall 21.5cm (8½in) thick. Some bricks will have to be cut to fit and the wall will need a coping.

Flemish bond

This bond looks similar and again involves some brick cutting. It too will need a coping, perhaps of brick set on edge as a 'soldier' course.

Stone walls

If you plan to build a 'free-standing' wall which is only one stone thick, bear in mind that, due to the unevenness of most stone, you will only achieve one 'fair' face, with the back of the wall ending up quite uneven.

For a 'free-standing' stone wall, you should consider building a double wall, the front skin being in stone with a backing made of 10cm (4in) concrete blocks (or more for stone); this would be classed as a composite wall. It would need a foundation twice as wide as before and it could also be used, in many cases, as a retaining wall.

Where there is an ample supply of stone and plenty space, a dry 'free-standing' wall can be built like the one illustrated above. Unlike the previous walls, this does not use mortar, nor need a concrete foundation.

Retaining walls

In all cases these should be at least 21.5cm (8½in) thick although if they are only two or three courses high they could be thinner. In most cases, the back of the wall will be against soil and out of sight so you could use concrete blocks instead of bricks or stone, because they are both cheaper and quicker to lay. It would also mean, however, that effectively you would be building up two walls side by side with no bricks or stones going through from front to back (except at the top) to bond the walls together. You should,

therefore, incorporate steel ties as you go, laid across from front to back wherever two courses coincide. As you near the top of the wall, you should change back to brick or stone for the back of the wall so that the concrete blocks are not visible.

Walls which hold back a bank of soil may be blocking the natural movement of water. Where this is the case, create 'weepholes' in the lower part of the wall, perhaps by merely leaving out the mortar from some of the vertical joints so that water can seep through. Remember, though, that these holes must go through

A strong retaining wall

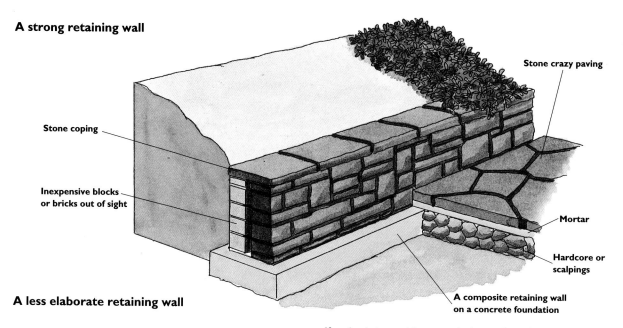

Stone coping

Inexpensive blocks or bricks out of sight

Stone crazy paving

Mortar

Hardcore or scalpings

A composite retaining wall on a concrete foundation

A less elaborate retaining wall

If paving is to go right up to the base of a wall, make sure that the wall foundation has been set low enough.

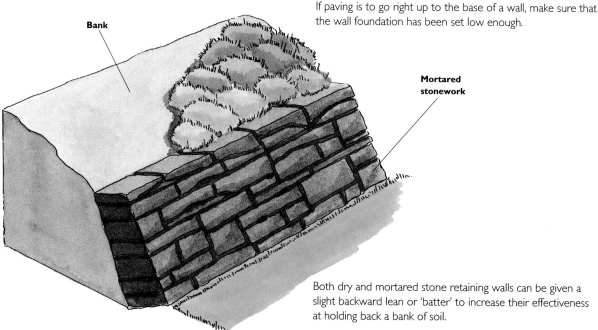

Bank

Mortared stonework

Both dry and mortared stone retaining walls can be given a slight backward lean or 'batter' to increase their effectiveness at holding back a bank of soil.

both skins of the wall. It would also be prudent to add some stones behind the wall to assist drainage and to filter out any soil or debris which might otherwise block the weepholes.

Screen block walls

These walls are built from square, 'see-through' concrete blocks measuring about 30cm (12in) square. They can be bought as a kit with their own pilaster blocks (for constructing the piers) and moulded coping. The blocks are not bonded but are merely stacked on top of one another and, although the construction technique is similar to that used for a brick or concrete block wall, you might find it more difficult to master.

To make a more attractive screen block wall, you could use brick or stone piers, and start with a low brick or stone wall. When the wall itself is complete, finish off with a more attractive coping than the standard concrete one. It will be important to bond the blocks to the piers using some steel ties between the two for extra stability.

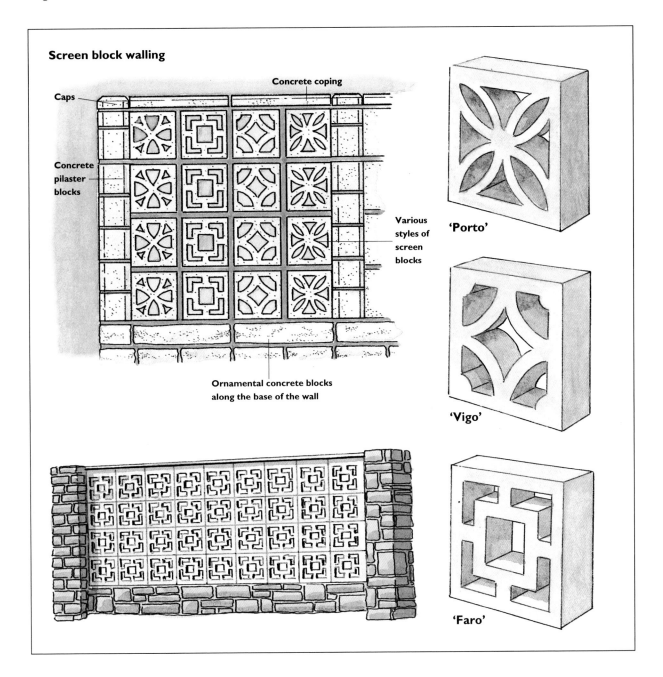

Screen block walling

Caps

Concrete coping

Concrete pilaster blocks

Various styles of screen blocks

Ornamental concrete blocks along the base of the wall

'Porto'

'Vigo'

'Faro'

Fences, screens and trellis

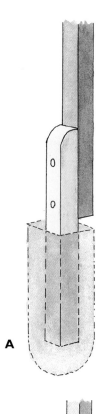

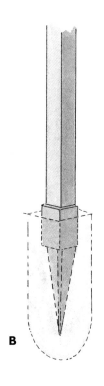

A

B

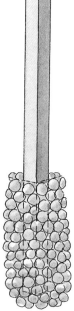

Different methods of post fixing

Posts can be fixed into the ground in a number of ways:

A. Bolted to a concrete fencing spur which is concreted into the ground.

B. Inserted into a metal post socket which is concreted into the ground.

C. Inserted into well-rammed stones or hardcore.

C

Erecting a panel fence

To erect a panel fence, in addition to the panels you will need pressure-treated posts 7.5cm or 10cm (3in or 4in) square and at least 60cm (2ft) taller than your panels (more in steeply sloping gardens), and post spurs or sockets made of concrete or metal, or simply a backfill of hardcore and stones.

Start by marking with pegs and string the line you intend the fence to take (if it is a boundary fence, make sure that you and your neighbours agree on the fence line before you go any further). Then, starting at the highest point, put in the first post on your side of the line, checking that it is perfectly vertical with a plumb-line or spirit level and that about 7.5cm (3in) will protrude above the panel. The method you choose to fix your posts into the ground will depend on the ground conditions and on how exposed your garden is to strong winds. Concrete spurs or metal sockets concreted or simply driven into the ground will be secure; these allow you to use shorter posts than if you insert the posts themselves into the ground secured with hardcore rammed round the base, in which case you should always try to have at least 45cm (18in) of post in the ground.

Next, place a couple of bricks or blocks on the ground in line with the string, and perfectly level so that they can support the fence panel horizontally while you offer it up to the post. You should find that you can slide the fence panel over the bricks and snugly up against the post. Fix the panel to the post with nails or special 'U'-shaped brackets, and support the unattached end of the panel with a temporary wooden stay while you insert the next post, which must be positioned tight up against the free end of the panel. Once you have fixed the panel to the second post, knock out the bricks, leaving the panel suspended just above ground level, then repeat the process for the subsequent panels and posts.

If the ground undulates you may have to vary the relative height of each panel and perhaps use longer or shorter posts to compensate and keep the top of the fence level. You can finish off your fence by adding post caps and by painting the whole thing with a plant-safe wood stain and preservative, perhaps in a soft chocolate brown or olive green – two colours which provide a suitable backdrop to most plants.

If you are replacing an old fence but find that the concrete post-supports are impossible to remove, start the job with a 'doctored' half panel. This will then ensure that all the subsequent new posts will end up being positioned between the old ones.

Erecting a closeboard fence

This type of fence is usually built from a kit. The guidelines for post length and fixing are the same as for panel fencing (above) although, because the fence will slope up or down with major changes in ground levels, the posts can all be the same length. You will first need to assemble a framework of arris rails (triangular lengths of wood) and posts, 10cm or 15cm (4in or 6in) square, which already have two or three mortice holes into which the tapered ends of the arris rails will fit - one at the top, one near the bottom and perhaps one in the middle. You also need 'gravel' boards to run horizontally along the base of the fence and 'feather-edge' boards of the appropriate size to form the fence panels.

Post caps

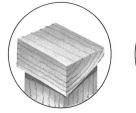

A wooden cap deflects rain and protects the top of the fencing post.

This type of post cap can be made from roofing felt or, better still, from aluminium sheeting which could be painted the same colour as the frame.

Various fence fixings

Overlapping panel fence

A 'U'-shaped bracket can be used to fix the top, middle and bottom of the panel to its post

Closeboard fence

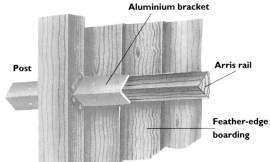

Aluminium bracket

Post

Arris rail

Feather-edge boarding

Panel fence

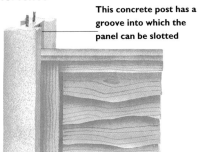

This concrete post has a groove into which the panel can be slotted

Begin making the framework for the closeboard fence with a string line to determine the fence line and your first post fixed firmly in the ground, with any mortice holes pointing along the line. Also dig the next post hole but merely rest the post in it, then take two arris rails and fix them, parallel to the ground, into the top and bottom holes of the first and second posts to produce a rather unstable framework. Fix the second post firmly then continue to build subsequent sections in the same way until the whole fence framework is complete and rigid. These posts must be vertical in both directions, so use a spirit level.

Next, rake the ground level between each post and then nail the gravel boards horizontally between the posts at ground level. The bottom of each vertical feather-edge board will rest on these so you must make sure that they strike a smooth line along the entire length of the fence. After you have done this, nail the feather-edge boards vertically to the arris rails, overlapping each by at least 1cm (½in). The top arris rail should be about 10cm (4in) below the top of these boards and the post tops about 5cm (2in) above. On steeply sloping ground where the possibility of uneven measurement could arise, the top and the bottom of each feather-edge board could be cut at an appropriate angle in order to produce an extra neat finish.

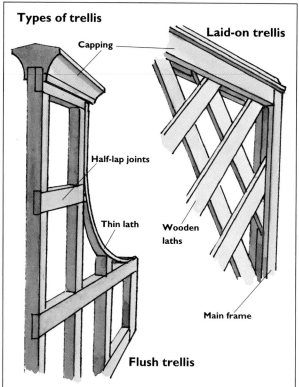

Types of trellis

Capping

Laid-on trellis

Half-lap joints

Thin lath

Wooden laths

Main frame

Flush trellis

Flush trellis is usually made from planed timber and would be more difficult to make than laid-on trellis which can be made from planed or sawn timber.

Fixing trellis to a wall

This trellis is hinged so that it, together with the plants it supports, can be swung out of the way to allow easy access to the wall.

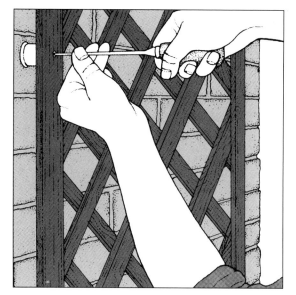

Leaving a gap between the trellis and the wall gives climbers a better chance of attaching themsleves by twining round the support; it also encourages air circulation.

Types of fence or screen

Chevron pattern using laths on a main frame

Bamboo screen

Round topped picket fence

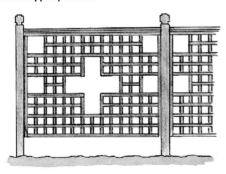

This 'squared' laid-on trellis has had some pieces cut out to produce a simple but effective pattern. Never over-do this, otherwise the panel may become too flimsy

Woven panels

These are a good choice for country gardens and include 'woven wattle' hurdles made from horizontally woven hazel (*Corylus*) or willow (*Salix*) branches, peeled reed screens using reeds woven vertically, and heather panels. You would normally erect these by wiring them top and bottom, to stout, treated, rustic poles placed at regular, measured intervals, temporarily supporting the panels on bricks, as described above, so that they are held 5cm (2in) or so off the ground. Using stout galvanised wire, the panels are attached tightly to the rustic poles top and bottom, the wire being pulled as tight as possible before being twisted closed. A fencing staple hammered into the post will prevent the wire from slipping down. These panels are not very suitable for exposed gardens as they have a tendency to be blown over.

Bamboo

Rolls of split cane are available but are not self-supporting. To erect these you would need a system of stout uprights (rustic or 'sawn') supporting two or three tightly strained, horizontal, galvanized wires to coincide with the binding wires running through the rolls of bamboo. The bamboo panels are then hung on these wires and attached at frequent intervals using thinner wire ties. It would be wise to suspend this screen slightly above the ground to prevent it from becoming water soaked which would lead to rotting. It is not a particularly durable type of fence.

Trellis

There are two main types of trellis – 'laid-on' and 'flush'. Laid-on trellis is easy to make using lengths of lath or timber about 2.5 x 1.5cm (1 x ¾in). You simply lay a matrix of laths on top of one another to produce a pattern and then nail them together. Square or diamond shapes are the most popular and easiest to make. If you use stout laths like tile battens, your finished panel may be rigid enough to fix directly onto timber posts. If the laths are relatively flimsy, finish your trellis panel off with a rigid frame around the outside before mounting it on posts. Some of the most interesting yet practical designs are based on a straightforward squared pattern with pieces cut or left out to create shaped holes or tops. Curved tops can also be achieved in most types of trellis. The timber must be thoroughly treated with preservative and can, like fencing, be stained a colour.

Flush trellis

For this you will need thicker strips of planed or 'prepared' timber rather than rough sawn, at least 3.5cm (1¼in) thick (and a similar width) because each cross-joint or intersection is to be created by a half-lap joint. This involves carefully cutting out a segment halfway through each of two pieces of wood so that they can join flush and, ideally, be screwed (or possibly nailed) together. This takes a good deal more time and effort than making laid-on trellis and is, therefore, probably best reserved for more architectural projects where the trellis is not used for (and hidden by) plants but is a feature in its own right.

Pergolas, arches and decking

Sawn timber pergolas

Cap

The top of the post has had deep grooves cut out in to which the other timbers can fit

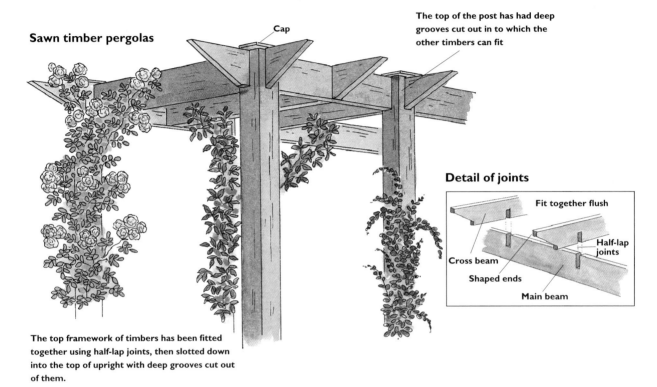

Detail of joints

Fit together flush

Half-lap joints

Cross beam

Shaped ends

Main beam

The top framework of timbers has been fitted together using half-lap joints, then slotted down into the top of upright with deep grooves cut out of them.

There are two main forms of timber that are suitable for the construction of pergolas, arches, decking and other similar garden structures: these are 'rustic' and 'sawn' timber.

'Rustic' poles

These are frequently made of pine, and are simply young trees which have been stripped of their bark and then pressure-treated with preservative. Irrespective of length, the poles are gauged by their top diameter (the diameter tends to vary along the length) and for most 'rustic' garden construction projects you would use uprights which have top diameters of 7.5–10cm (3–4in) and crosspoles with top diameters of 5–7.5cm (2–3in), but the latter could be thicker if they had to span a distance of more than say, 2.4m (8 ft).

Fixing into the ground

Although poles can simply be concreted in, this may encourage decay at ground level so it is preferable to set them as deeply as possible in holes in the ground and fill with well-rammed hardcore.

Joining poles

Bringing together two rounded sections does not produce a stable join because the area of contact between them is so small. Wherever possible, cut out a small, shallow section of pole to produce a limited flat surface so that the point of contact is increased. The best tools for doing this are a panel saw and chisel. Ring-shanked nails are better than smooth, or even galvanized ones because, once they have been banged into the wood, they will not come out. Treat all the cut ends and joints with extra preservative and if your poles have not been pressure treated with preservative, give the bottom part of each pole a particularly thorough dose.

Sawn timber

This is the most useful form of timber for constructing pergolas and arches which are not 'rustic' in style. A selection of planks, strips and posts of pressure-treated softwood can be joined to produce all manner of complex and attractive structures. The most common joints used are half-lap and mortice and will usually require fixing together with screws, bolts or nails. Nearly all these structures will depend upon having their uprights fixed very firmly in the ground for good stability and, whenever possible, incorporate into the design of your structure some sort of cross-bracing to add further to its strength.

Decking

For this you would also use sawn timber. The main supporting framework comprises a series of joists at least 15 × 5cm (6 × 2in) with slightly thinner joists, 10 × 5cm (4 × 2in) filling in and spanning the shorter distances between. The complexity of your completed frame will depend upon the pattern of the decking that you have planned to use. You would normally set this completed frame on top of bricks or blocks with a piece of damp-proof membrane between to stop rising damp.

Decking planks are available in several sizes but on average are 10–15cm (4–6in) wide by about 2cm (¾in) thick, and need to be supported at least every 50cm (20in) so that they do not warp or give. Leave a gap of about 1cm (⅜in) between each plank so that water can drain away quickly, otherwise the decking could become very slippery. Mark out where each plank should go on the framework or use a spacer to keep all the gaps parallel. If you have to use one odd-sized plank to cover the distance, try to work this into the centre rather than have it down one edge. Although nails are normally used to fix down decking, you could use brass or 'bright' countersunk screws with screw cups for constructions using the much more decorative (and more expensive) hardwood decking. Make any handrails or balustrades from planed wood which will be relatively free from splinters. All your finished projects can be stained afterwards using a colour which either matches existing features around the garden or the timber in your house.

Decking patterns and joists

This is the simplest arrangement of joists for decking planks which all run in the same direction.

This diagonal arrangement of decking planks will require a slightly more complex arrangement of joists.

An extra strong diagonal joist is needed for the joist frame of this particular decking pattern.

A small 'rustic' arch made with peeled, pressure-treated poles

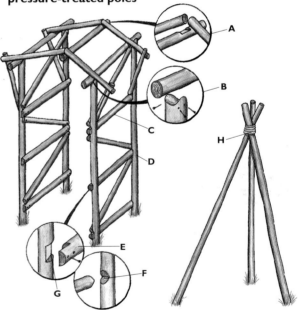

KEY

A. An arrangement of joints to produce a snug fit

B. Grooved joint

C. Poles with a top diameter of about 5cm (2in)

D. Poles with a top diameter of about 7.5cm (3in)

E. Galvanized or ring-shanked nails

F. Wedge joint

G. Shallow half-lap joint

H. This simple arrangement of three stout, rustic poles will provide support for climbing plants. Use pressure-treated poles with a top diameter of about 4–5cm (1½–2in)

Water features

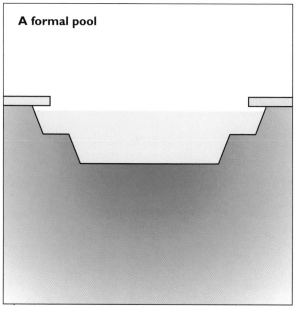

A formal pool

It is vital that the edges of this type of pool are perfectly level.

Various water features are discussed within the pages of this book, and all of them rely on some method of containing the water and, in some cases, moving it around. There are several different ways of achieving these effects but the success of any water feature will depend, at least in part, on choosing the most appropriate materials and equipment. Features with moving water should, ideally, be constructed within an all-embracing water-tight structure so that if water should leak from one part of the feature into another, it is not lost from the overall system. This is particularly important since all the features rely on recirculating the same water over and over again and any loss would soon be noticed. It is most important to make the water-tight area or shell large enough to accommodate the whole water feature.

Liners

There are two main problems with liners – the possibility of punctures, and the fact that they are often

Constructing a pool

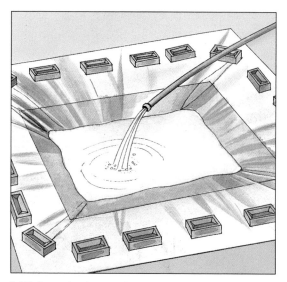

1. After ensuring that the top of the excavation is perfectly level, and after checking for any sharp objects, which should be removed, lay in the liner with, if possible, a 'felt' underlay. You should leave at least 30cm (12in) of overhang all round the edge. This can be held in place temporarily with bricks.

2. Fill the pool with water, but make sure that none of the bricks falls in and damages the liner.

visible in the finished feature. In a straightforward, formal garden pond this may not be too serious but in a feature that is supposed to look natural, it could be a nuisance. The object is to install the liner in such a way that it can do its job efficiently, but to disguise it using your chosen building materials.

All liners will last longer if they are protected from sharp objects and strong sunlight. One way you can achieve this is first to line a well-compacted excavation with either a special geotechnic felt underlay or a smooth 2cm (¾in) layer of mortar made from 1 part cement + 8 parts of soft sand. Once this has set you then place the liner on top and cover it with a further 2.5cm (1in) or so of mortar. You will now be able to build a feature within this area leaving the protected liner to work behind the scenes.

Butyl liner This is probably the strongest, longest lasting and most expensive of all commonly available liners. It is a fairly thick, synthetic rubber sheet which is usually black. It can be used for all sorts of water features but although it is difficult to puncture it is not ideal for rocky water projects unless it is protected in some way. If used in a very small area, say less than about 1.5m (5ft) across, the folds that arise from fitting it may prove difficult to flatten. Pipework can easily be plumbed in and out of a butyl liner

HOW MUCH?

Liners are usually sold as a rectangular or square sheet or cut off a wide roll, so it is very easy to ensure that you buy the correct length. The following formula should help you to assess the overall length and width you will require:

overall length = length of pool/feature + twice maximum depth + twice any overlap at the edges
overall width = width of pool/feature + the depth and overlap measurements as above

using standard, plastic domestic pipework and fittings. In the event of damage, it can usually be repaired using butyl patches and vulcanizing fluid.

Bonded PVC products These are produced from a double thickness of PVC with a terylene net welded inbetween. The net provides some extra strength but PVC is much more easily damaged than butyl, will eventually become brittle where it is exposed to sunlight and is more difficult to repair. It is, however, less expensive and is available in a variety of colours.

PVC sheeting (1000-gauge or more) This has similar properties to bonded PVC but is not as strong. It is considerably cheaper but not usually available in quite as many colours.

3. Trim off the excess liner, leaving not less than 100mm (4in) all round to fit under the paving.

4. Add the paving, perhaps with some foundation material so that, if possible, it will end up just below the level of the adjoining grass.

Rock pools and waterfalls

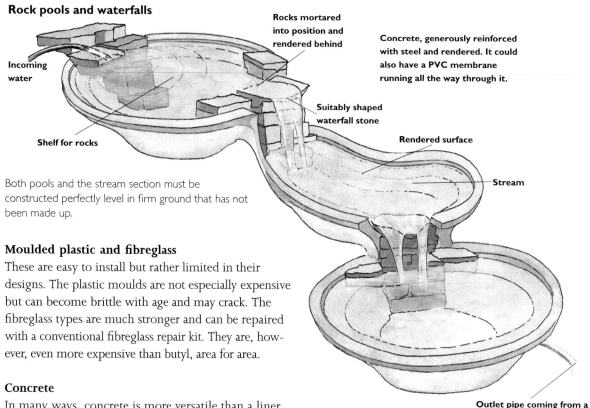

Incoming water

Shelf for rocks

Rocks mortared into position and rendered behind

Concrete, generously reinforced with steel and rendered. It could also have a PVC membrane running all the way through it.

Suitably shaped waterfall stone

Rendered surface

Stream

Outlet pipe coming from a submersible pump in the bottom pond

Both pools and the stream section must be constructed perfectly level in firm ground that has not been made up.

Moulded plastic and fibreglass

These are easy to install but rather limited in their designs. The plastic moulds are not especially expensive but can become brittle with age and may crack. The fibreglass types are much stronger and can be repaired with a conventional fibreglass repair kit. They are, however, even more expensive than butyl, area for area.

Concrete

In many ways, concrete is more versatile than a liner, especially for rock and water features. It is, however, less convenient to use, harder work to install and may crack if not reinforced. It is better suited to a feature which has sides that slope rather than one with vertical sides.

The mix will consist of:

1 part of cement + 6 parts of all-in ballast + water. The idea is to produce a stiff mix that will stack up the sides rather than slopping to the bottom. Place about 5–7cm (2¾ in) of this concrete evenly over the excavation, tamping it thoroughly into position with a wooden float or block of wood, before laying a matrix of steel rods or wire over the surface. Then add a further 7.5cm (3in) or so of concrete and tamp it into position. In unstable or clay soil use a greater thickness of concrete. Cover it with a thin PVC sheet for a day or two to allow it to cure before brushing in a rendering mix to an initial thickness of about 1cm (⅜in).

The mix will consist of:

1 part of cement + 6-8 parts of sharp sand + a waterproofing additive + water.

Mix this to a paste-like consistency, so that it is easy to apply with a stiff hard brush. Apply the first layer then cover with PVC for about 24 hours before repeating the process with the second layer. This will make the concrete waterproof. There are also various products available, either clear or coloured, which can sprayed or painted on to increase the water-tightness still further. Do not fill your feature with water until the rendering has completely set or any waterproofing product has completely dried.

If you have used no additives or paints, you could find that free lime leaches out of the concrete into the water, killing pond life. To reduce this, spray or paint the surface with a solution of sodium silicate (water glass) which will turn the calcium into a protective, colourless glaze.

COMBINED CONSTRUCTION

If you feel that concrete would suit your needs best but are worried about cracking, very carefully incorporate a whole sheet of PVC between two layers of concrete, in the same way as the steel, but at least 3.5cm (1¼in) beneath the top surface. You would not, in this case, have to render the concrete.

Choosing a pump

The pump you use is likely to be a submersible type and, therefore, will operate under water. There is always a limit to the height (head) to which a pump can push water. As this height increases, along with pipe length, so the flow decreases and the effect can diminish along with it. There is usually a performance table on the side of the pump's packaging to indicate this. One way of visualizing what different flow rates (expressed in gallons or litres per hour) look like is to run your bath tap into a bucket of a known capacity and time, at various tap settings, and to note how quickly the bucket fills up. This can easily be translated into litres or gallons per hour and will therefore help you to select the most appropriate pump for the size and shape of your water feature.

It is always wise to select a pump that is more powerful than you require and to use a flow valve to control its output. As time goes by you will then be able to compensate for any reduction in performance due to dirt or wear and tear by opening the valve filter a little further.

A rock-lined pool

Stones can be mortared onto the inside of a concrete pool or stacked carefully within a liner.

A child-safe water feature

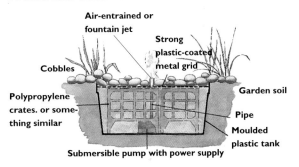

Much of the water is out of reach in an underground reservoir.

Creating a formal cascade

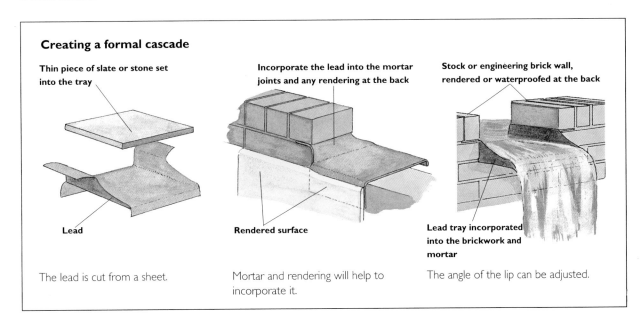

The lead is cut from a sheet.

Mortar and rendering will help to incorporate it.

The angle of the lip can be adjusted.

Rock gardens

The main purpose of a rock garden is, of course, to provide an attractive feature in which you can grow a collection of alpine plants. Alpines need an open position, away from trees, and a fairly sunny aspect, so try to position your rock garden accordingly. Avoid weed-infested or waterlogged ground and try to ensure that the soil you use to build up the terraces is well-drained, weed-free and, ideally, alkaline rather than acid. Also bear in mind that the rock garden should appear to be a natural feature, and so will look better emerging from shrubs or as part of a bank than being tacked onto a fence or garden wall.

Planning

A rock garden can be planned in general terms. You can decide where the main outcrops will be and whether there will be any steps, areas of scree and so on, but the rest can only fall in to place once you have the individual rocks in front of you. You can, however, build a small model in a box or on a tray using small pieces of broken stone or bark to represent rocks and have this nearby while you are actually building the rock garden.

Type of rock

To be truly authentic you should use only the type of rock that occurs naturally in your area but, in reality, you can use almost any type of rock you choose within the confines of your garden. Although rocks can be viewed and purchased in a garden centre or specialist's yard, you will find it far more useful to see some completed rock gardens before making your choice. The stone you choose will determine the style of your rock garden, so choose with care. Flattish, craggy rocks, such as slate, will produce a rather flat rock garden whereas large, cube-shaped pieces will be comparatively easy to build upwards to create height. Avoid very soft sandstone because it may break up in frost. If you are planning to have a path, steps and scree in your rock garden, choose a rock which is available as paving, broken scree and gravel as well as the rockery stone so that it all matches.

How much stone?

One way of arriving at an approximate quantity (stone is usually sold by weight) is to reckon that you could well be using pieces of stone which are, on average, about the size of a 50kg (110lb) bag of cement and would, therefore, weigh about the same. You can then try to envisage how many such pieces of stone you would need, multiply by 50 (or 110) and arrive at a total weight, probably in tonnes (tons). Alternatively, you could plan to start with smaller pieces, say the equivalent of half a bag of cement, and calculate from that basis.

A typical flat rock

Flat rocks like this one will tend to produce a relatively low, flat rock garden.

Block-shaped rocks (above and below)

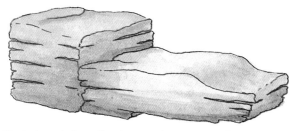

Block-shaped pieces like the two above are usually easy to place on top of one another, producing a steep rock garden.

Creating fissures

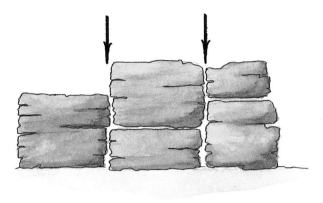

When you build rocks on top of one another, do not bond them like bricks in a wall, but, instead, create vertical joints.

Strata

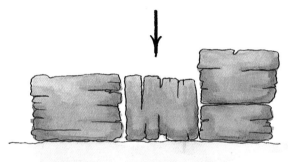

Do check each rock for strata lines so that these can all be arranged in the same plane throughout the rock garden.

Strata

Many types of rock have lines of weakness called strata running through them. In nature, these lines all run more or less the same way throughout huge outcrops or boulders of which you could only ever fit a tiny portion in your garden. If your rock garden is to look natural, you should endeavour to arrange the rocks with their strata all running in the same direction – that is to say, usually horizontally but with a slight backward lean.

Another point to remember when trying to make your rock garden looks as natural as possible is that if you pile rocks on top of one another to create height, you will need to line up all the vertical joints above one another as if they were a natural fissure. Do not attempt to bond or stagger rocks like bricks in a wall; the result was not looking realistic.

Steps and scree areas

You should create an opportunity to increase the density of your rock arrangement by creating small, 'rustic' flights of steps here and there. In another area, you could have a significant sweep of broken stones and gravel, perhaps to a depth of 7.5–10cm (3–4in) to provide a scree for alpines which are suited to these conditions.

A scree for alpines
This area of scree has a layer of drainage material at the bottom, well-drained compost and a mulch of stones on top. This should prevent waterlogging from occuring and help the plants to grow successfully.

LIFTING

Adopt some of the following methods for moving heavy rocks around:

- Rollers, about eight: 60cm (2ft) lengths of smooth 'rustic' pole beneath a plank
- Two-wheeled sack trolley and planks
- Iron bar or strong pole used as a lever
- Winch for dragging very large rocks short distances
- Thick sheet of PVC for dragging rocks across lawns
- Finally, if in doubt, roll rather than lift rocks and wear thick gloves

Building a rock outcrop

1. Fit rocks together as naturally as possible, creating nooks and crevices wherever you can.

2. It may be necessary to chip pieces off here and there to help some of the rock fit together better.

3. Pack soil or compost firmly behind the rocks so that it will not sink or wash out easily.

4. Finish off with a layer of sterilized compost and, after planting, a mulch of gravel or grit.

Building into a natural bank

First make sure the bank is completely free of weeds. Start a little way forward from the bottom of the bank by placing one of your largest rocks at an angle of about 45° rather than parallel to the bank and with its strata more or less horizontal. Incorporate a slight backward lean at the same time. You can then build back from this point in two directions, using similar sized rocks so that, in a short distance, you will run into the bottom of the bank to create a good sized, wedge-shaped outcrop. Use either soil from the bank you are building into, or some imported soil to fill this area right to the top, compacting it as you go. You should end up with a flat plateau of rock which slopes back very gently.

You can now build further, similar outcrops on either side before moving up and onto the new plateau and starting again a little way back from the edge so that you have some planting space before the next row of rocks. Be as imaginative as you can and avoid straight rows of rocks which would end up looking more like terraced walls.

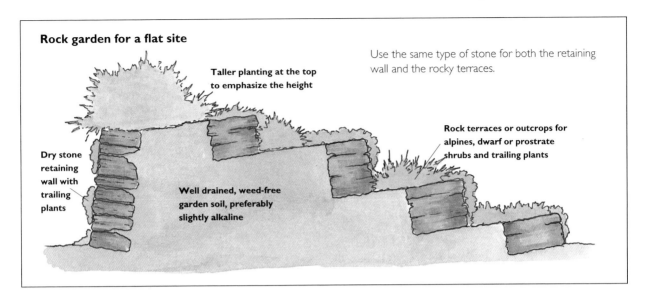

Rock garden for a flat site

Use the same type of stone for both the retaining wall and the rocky terraces.

Taller planting at the top to emphasize the height

Rock terraces or outcrops for alpines, dwarf or prostrate shrubs and trailing plants

Dry stone retaining wall with trailing plants

Well drained, weed-free garden soil, preferably slightly alkaline

A rock garden on flat ground

It is possible to create a rock garden on a site that was initially flat, but it will require considerable preparation. You will have to elevate an area of garden with the help of a smallish retaining wall which will then form the back of the rock garden. If the wall is likely to be visible then build it from natural stone. However, for any parts which are not visible, use a less expensive material, such as concrete blocks.

Starting at ground level and well to the front of the area, set your first tier of rocks all the way round, gradually changing to walling stone as you go around the back. Once this bottom ring of stone is complete, fill up with suitable soil and compact it to produce a

reasonably firm terrace on which you can build the next tier. At the back you will have to build right on top of the stones you have just laid to create a wall, but, to the sides and at the front, set your next row of stones well back so that you have space for planting in front of them. Once again, be as imaginative as you can and avoid making too uniform and symmetrical a structure.

Planting

Apart from alpines, most of which are small and low-growing, incorporate some dwarf shrubs, slow-growing conifers and a few specimen or dot plants. The apparent height of your rock garden can be increased very effectively by using one or two larger plants, possibly conifers, near the top and keeping to very flat or low plants around the bottom. There are many alpine bulbs worth growing and if your rock garden has plenty of crevices, and shady nooks as well as hot sunny plateaux, you will be able to grow a vast range of alpines in quite a small area.

Building a rock outcrop

The lower terrace or tier of an outcrop is built first and compacted thoroughly

The second terrace or tier is built on top of the first

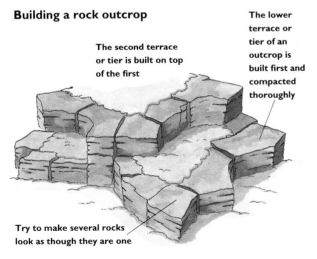

Try to make several rocks look as though they are one

Match together the various angles on each rock in order to create natural and interesting changes of direction.

A GROTTO

This would ideally take the form of a small cave, perhaps with a pool at its entrance. To create a feature like this you would need at least one large, relatively long, flat stone as a lintel and perhaps some steel bars to support a roof of stone and earth. If there is to be a pool, construct this first using some steel-reinforced concrete then build your grotto and the adjacent rock garden around it.

Planting plans

Skilful arrangement of
plants for height,
shape, colour and
texture can produce
some very attractive
and interesting
borders around
your garden.

Introducing plants

A successful planting scheme is a pleasing arrangement of plants that thrive in the local climatic and soil conditions and harmonize with the overall style of the house and garden. It should require only as much attention as the owner wishes to give it.

There is always plenty of choice when it comes to selecting plants to fill a particular space in the garden. You can choose plants for their decorative flowers, fragrance, evergreen or variegated foliage, coloured stems and bark, fruits and berries, their ability to climb or trail, or perhaps their culinary value.

For cultural reasons, some plants need a special environment: many alpines need a rockery, scree bed or sink garden, bog plants damp soil and aquatic plants water. In a small garden, you may not have room for more than a few plants of each type, all arranged in terms of height, spread and habit.

For a small garden, choose trees carefully, with the emphasis on those that are relatively slow growing. There are also many bushy trees that are more like large shrubs, and, likewise, some garden shrubs can be trained as trees. If using trees to add height and structure to a shrub border, position them at the back, with more decorative plants in front. A tree chosen specially for its ornamental bark, however, should be given pride of place in the centre of a lawn, for example. When using trees for screening, remember that, given time, they will block out more and more light as they mature, and this will begin to affect the performance of plants around them.

With so many interesting and beautiful climbers available, it would be a shame not to have at least two or three. Climbing plants have different ways of attaching themselves and all, except those with suction pads, need wires or trellis. Some, including roses, jasmine and honeysuckle, need tying-in, but others like clematis and passiflora will twine round their support with only a minimum of help. Climbers with suckers, however, like *Parthenocissus* and *Hedera*, should not be grown up rendered or decorated houses.

Climatic conditions

Some plants are affected by frost so, if you live in a notoriously cold area, stick to hardy types. For example, *Escallonia* is nearly always cut down to ground level by frosts and has to grow again each spring, never reaching more than 1.2m (4ft), rather than its height of 3m (10ft) in mild areas. Other factors affecting plant growth include salt-laden winds near the coast, hot, dry conditions and windy, exposed sites.

Soil conditions

Soil conditions are a major influence on what you can and cannot grow. Is your soil light and sandy, wet and heavy, with a high clay content, or, ideally, a loam? Is it acid (with a low pH), neutral or alkaline (with a high pH)? Plants like dianthus and some alpines may grow poorly in acid soil and, similarly, alkaline soil is not suitable for rhododendrons, summer-flowering heathers, camellias or any other ericaceous (acid-loving) plants, although some plants will grow but not thrive in alkaline soil; many, like *Magnolia soulangeana*, start to produce pale-coloured leaves. By looking around your own locality, you will soon get to know which plants grow well in the local type of soil.

Aspect

The aspect of a border, and thus the amount of sun it receives, depends on its orientation. Areas beneath trees, however, will often be in the shade whatever the aspect, although this type of shade could be much less dense (but drier) than that created by a building or fence. Select plants appropriate to the light levels of each border; low levels tend to inhibit flowering, as with wisterias, and sometimes growth, while some foliage loses its bright colour. A good choice for a shady spot is *Sambucus nigra* 'Marginata', a brightly variegated elder, which will grow to half its height under large trees but retains its striking coloration. Roses are usually planted in full sun, but they will do almost as well in constant shade (away from trees).

Rates of growth

It is hard to tell, apart from by reading labels, how high or wide containerized plants from garden centres are likely to grow. If you examine trees and shrubs very closely and measure the current year's growth, you can assume that they will continue to grow at this rate (given suitable conditions), at least for the next few years. This should give you some idea of where to put a particular plant and how many plants you need. Sooner or later, however, you may have to intervene with pruning. Most herbaceous plants, bulbs and annuals that start from nothing each spring and complete their growth and flowering by the autumn are much more predictable than trees and shrubs.

Year-round interest

Colour and interest are often at a low ebb during winter, although there may be other times during summer when the number of plants in flower is quite small. You can easily remedy this by either using some bedding plants or by adding one or two plants which will flower at those specific times. For winter interest, the first step is to include a scattering of evergreens throughout the garden, some of which could be conifers or shrubs with variegated or silver-coloured foliage. To make the garden more lively in summer, either plant herbaceous bedding plants or add one or two shrubs which flower at the required time.

Habit

There are many different types of plants, all with different habits, including plants that climb, plants that creep along the ground (prostrate), plants that go straight up, often as a single column (fastigiate), and plants that hang down.

Fastigiate plants like *Juniperus scopulorum* 'Skyrocket' and spiky plants like *Yucca* are particularly striking in habit, along with prostrate ground-cover plants. Try a combination of the almost prostrate conifer *Juniperus squamata* 'Blue Carpet' growing at the base of the variegated *Yucca filamentosa*. Another good association is *Santolina chamaecyparissus* in front of *Lonicera nitida* 'Baggeson's Gold': this produces a soft (and rather untidy) mass of gold and silver foliage. A collection of ornamental grasses can be very effective because they are similar in habit, yet they vary in height and have subtle variations in texture and colour.

Some plants, however, are best used as specimen plants with a carpet of ground cover underneath. Examples of these include shrubs or small trees like *Magnolia stellata*, some of the smaller species of *Acer* and small weeping plants like *Salix caprea* 'Kilmarnock'.

Colour co-ordination

Although colour is a matter of personal taste, there are a few general guidelines to help plan the colour schemes of your borders.

Colours should be chosen to either harmonize or contrast, depending on the effect and mood you want to create. Mellow, harmonious colours such as blue, green, white and silver used together create a tranquil impression of space, while bright, contrasting colours like red, orange and yellow serve to liven up a border, making it seem busy and often smaller in size. A predominance of blue will make a border seem further away, while areas of red make it seem nearer. Do not forget the many different greens provided by foliage, including yellowy-green, silvery-green (as with *Helichrysum italicum*) and purple-green (as with the maroon-leafed *Heuchera* 'Palace Purple' and *Salvia officinalis* 'Purpurascens').

Try to avoid clashing colours such as pink and orange, or at least dilute them with green, white or grey (all neutral colours) to soften the impact. In a small garden it is not easy to avoid colour clashes because everything is at such close quarters, but try to arrange your planting so that any potentially clashing colours flower at different times.

Texture

The texture of a plant can perhaps be best appreciated from a distance. Some plants appear soft and misty, like *Santolina chamaecyparissus*, *Lonicera nitida* 'Baggeson's Gold', *Gypsophila* and *Thalictrum*, while others appear dense and statuesque, like *Viburnum davidii*, *Fatsia japonica* and rhododendrons. Aim at having a mixture of both, along with variations in habit and colour.

About the planting schemes

Rather than being definitive planting plans, the following are intended to inspire you to develop your own schemes. The plans can be used separately or combined in new and exciting ways with other plans and your own ideas to create highly personal plantings to suit the individual style and conditions of your garden. To help you do this, some of the illustrations show plants in flower, or berry, at the same time when they may not actually appear together in the garden. This has been done purely for illustrative purposes so as to give you some idea of what each plant might look like in its main season of interest.

In all cases, heights (H) and spreads (S) are intended as a rough guide, for your growing conditions may produce results different to the average. Note that plants classified as herbaceous are often commonly known as perennials or border plants.

MIXED SUNNY BORDER

This border is part of the garden design on page 42, but the plants will grow in any sheltered border that catches the sun for most of the day. The soil is neutral and reasonably well-drained. Any climbing plants will need some kind of support, such as a 'rustic' trellis, as seen here.

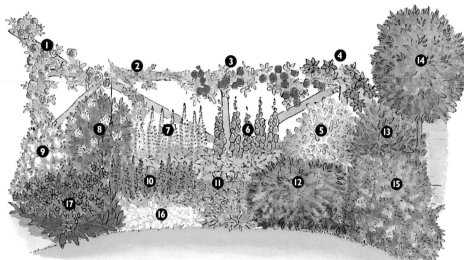

1 Rosa 'Zéphirine Drouhin' (climbing rose)
Deciduous climber – 1 plant
Thornless; flowers semi-double, rose-pink and fragrant, borne in summer. H 2.4–3m (8–10ft); S 2.4–3m (8–10ft).

2 Lonicera japonica 'Halliana' (Japanese honeysuckle)
Semi-evergreen climber – 1 plant
Vigorous, very hardy; flowers from summer to autumn; sweetly scented and creamy white, maturing to pale biscuit colour. H 2.4m (8ft); S 1.5m (5ft).

3 Rosa 'Guinée' (climbing rose)
Deciduous climber – 1 plant
Foliage fairly bold; deep reddish-black, scented flowers appear in summer; repeat flowering. H 2.4–3m (8–10ft); S 2.4–3m (8–10ft).

4 Clematis 'The President' (Patens Group)
Deciduous climber – 1 plant
Vigorous. Flowers purple suffused claret; produced on old and new wood from mid- to late summer. H 3m (10ft); S 3m (10ft).

5 Griselinia littoralis 'Variegata' (broadleaf)
Evergreen shrub – 1 plant
Leaves rounded, brightly variegated, green and white; fleshy. Susceptible to scorching from cold winds and hard frost. H 1.8m (6ft); S 1.2m (4ft).

6 Delphinium 'Blue Jay'
Herbaceous – Up to 3 plants
Flowers mid-blue with white eye, borne in summer. Dies back to ground level in winter. H 1.5m (5ft); S 50cm (20in).

7 Lupinus 'The Chatelaine' (lupin)
Herbaceous – Up to 3 plants
Flowers bi-coloured, pink and white, produced in mid-summer. H 1m (3ft 3in); S 50cm (20in).

8 Viburnum tinus
Evergreen shrub – 1 plant
Leaves very dark green; flowers produced from winter to early spring; fragrant and pinky-white. H 3m (10ft); S 1.8m (6ft).

9 Olearia x haastii (daisy bush)
Evergreen shrub – 1 plant
Upright habit becomes rounded with age. Leaves small, greyish-green; flowers white and daisy-like, produced in late summer. H 1.2m (4 ft); S 70–80cm (2ft 3in–2ft 9in).

10 Salvia nemorosa 'East Friesland' (sage)
Herbaceous – Up to 3 plants
Violet-blue flowers held on slender spikes appear in early summer. H 45cm (18in); S 25cm (10in).

11 Aster thomsonii 'Nanus' (Michaelmas daisy)
Herbaceous – Up to 3 plants
Leaves greyish-green, flowers lavender-blue, produced from late summer to early autumn. H 45cm (18in); S 25cm (10in).

12 Weigela florida 'Foliis Purpureis'
Deciduous shrub – 1 plant
Small, compact. Leaves dull purple; flowers produced in early summer; pink and held in clusters. H 1.2m (4ft); S 1.2–1.5m (4–5ft).

13 Viburnum farreri (syn. V. fragrans)
Deciduous shrub – 1 plant
Leaves green with bronzy tinge. Flowers from winter to early spring; pink, fragrant and held in small clusters on bare stems. H 2m (6ft 6in); S 1.2m (4ft).

14 Prunus x blireana (cherry)
Deciduous tree – 1 plant
Leaves bronze growing darker as summer progresses;. Blossom small, semi-double, deep pink, produced on leafless twiggy branches in spring. H 5m (16ft); S 4m (13ft).

15 Escallonia 'Apple Blossom'
Semi-evergreen shrub – 1 plant
Leaves glossy and aromatic; flowers pale pink, produced in profusion on arching stems from early to mid-summer. In sheltered, frost-free site: H 1.5m (5ft); S 1.5m (5ft).

16 Stachys byzantina 'Silver Carpet' (syn. S. lanata' Silver Carpet') (bunnies' ears/ lamb's tongue)
Semi-evergreen herbaceous – 3–5 plants
Leaves silver-grey and woolly, forming a creeping mat; non-flowering. H 15cm (6in); S 45cm (18in).

17 Lychnis arkwrightii (campion)
Herbaceous – 3 plants
Leaves deep maroon-purple; flowers intense scarlet, borne in mid-summer. Dies back in winter or early autumn after very dry summer. H 30cm (12in); S 25cm (10in).

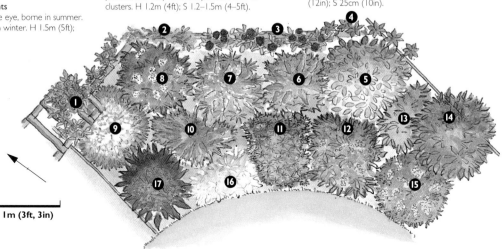

1m (3ft, 3in)

FRAGRANT SUNNY BORDER

This planting plan is from the garden design on page 60. All the plants, many of which are deliciously scented, will grow in a sunny border with neutral soil.

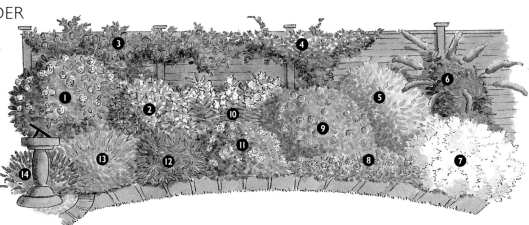

1 Viburnum carlesii
Deciduous shrub – 1 plant
Rounded. Foliage colours in autumn. Dense clusters of fragrant white flowers produced in spring. H 1.5m (5ft); S 1.5m (5ft).

2 Osmanthus heterophyllus 'Variegatus'
Evergreen shrub – 1 plant
Cream and green variegated, holly-like foliage. Flowers tiny, fragrant and white, produced in late summer. H 1.5m (5ft); S 1m (3ft 3in).

3 Rosa 'Compassion' (climbing rose)
Deciduous climber – 1 plant
Foliage glossy green. Flowers pale salmon-orange, very fragrant, produced in summer. H 2.4–3m (8–10ft); S 2.4–3m (8–10ft).

4 Jasminum officinale f. affine (syn. J. o. 'Grandiflorum') (summer flowering jasmine)
Semi-evergreen climber (depending on climate) – 1 plant
Very vigorous. Fresh green foliage. Small, white, very fragrant flowers borne in summer. H 2.4m (8ft); S 3m (10ft).

5 Philadelphus coronarius 'Aureus' (mock orange)
Deciduous shrub – 1 plant
Young foliage bright yellow fading to lime green. Flowers highly scented, produced in mid-summer. H 1.5m (5ft); S 1.2m (4ft).

6 Buddleja davidii 'Nanho Purple' (butterfly bush)
Deciduous shrub – 1 plant
Foliage grey-green. Flower panicles borne in summer; purple-red, fragrant and attractive to butterflies. H 1.5m (5ft); S 1.5m (5ft).

7 Santolina chamaecyparissus (cotton lavender)
Evergreen shrub – 1 to 2 plants
Silvery-white, woolly foliage. Flowers in summer; small, lemon-yellow and often removed. H 60cm (2ft); S 90cm (3ft).

8 Dianthus 'Mrs Pilkington' (garden pink)
Semi-evergreen herbaceous – 5 plants
Tufts of grey foliage persistent through winter. Flowers in early summer; rose pink, double and fragrant. H 30cm (12in); S 25cm (10in).

9 Rosa 'Mary Rose' (modern shrub rose)
Deciduous shrub – 1 plant
Plentiful foliage. Fragrant, flesh-pink and 'old rose' shaped flowers produced in summer. H 1.2–1.5m (4–5ft); S 1.2–1.5m (4–5ft).

10 Lilium regale (regal lily)
Bulb – 5 plants
Flowers produced in mid-spring; creamy-coloured, trumpet-shaped and very fragrant. H 1m (3ft 3in); s 25cm (10in).

11 Philadelphus 'Manteau d'Hermine' (dwarf mock orange)
Deciduous shrub – 1 plant
Compact. Small, double, fragrant white flowers produced in early summer. H 1m (3ft 3in); S 1m (3ft 3in).

12 Daphne odora 'Aureomarginata'
Evergreen shrub – 1 plant
Flowers small, pinky-white, highly scented, produced in very early spring. Highly poisonous red berries. H 1.2m (4ft); S 1.2m (4ft).

13 Lavandula angustifolia (old English lavender)
Semi-evergreen shrub – 1 plant
Foliage grey-green, needle-like. Spikes of lavender flowers from mid-summer onwards. Strongly aromatic. Clipped: H 1m (3ft 3in); S 1m (3ft 3in).

14 Lavandula angustifolia 'Hidcote' (old English lavender)
Semi-evergreen shrub – 1 to 3 plants
Flowers violet in dense compact spikes from mid-summer onwards. Can be used as informal hedge. H 60cm (2ft); S 45cm (18in).

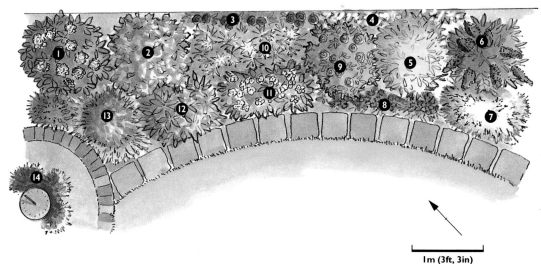

1m (3ft, 3in)

MIXED FOLIAGE BORDER

This border features in the garden design on page 24, but these plants will grow anywhere as long as the soil is a medium loam with a neutral pH. Evergreens provide winter interest, while the deciduous plants ensure seasonal variety. The climbing plants will need a fence or trellis for support.

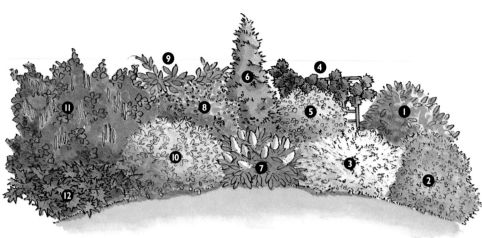

1 Viburnum tinus 'Variegatum'
Evergreen shrub – 1 plant
Rounded. Foliage dark green with bright yellow variegation. Flowers fragrant and whitish, produced in winter and early spring. H 2.4m (8ft); S 1.8m (6ft).

2 Ruta graveolens 'Jackman's Blue' (rue)
Semi-evergreen shrubby herb – 1 plant
Foliage striking blue, aromatic. Yellow flowers in summer. H 90cm (3ft); S 90cm (3ft).

3 Santolina chamaecyparissus (cotton lavender)
Evergreen shrub – 1 plant
Foliage silver; small, yellow flowers in summer can be removed. Tolerates wide range of conditions. H 60cm (2ft); S 90cm (3ft).

4 Vitis vinifera 'Purpurea' (grape vine)
Deciduous climber – 1 plant
Vigorous. Foliage greenish-purple in summer, deep plum by autumn. Requires training. H 2.4m (8ft); S 3m (10ft).

5 Eucalyptus gunnii (cider gum)
Evergreen tree/shrub – 1 plant
Juvenile foliage rounded, bright bluish-grey. Mature foliage pointed, less glaucous. Regular pruning restricts size and maintains juvenile foliage. If pruned back: H 1.5m (5ft); S 1.2m (4ft).

6 Chamaecyparis lawsoniana 'Columnaris Glauca' (Lawson cypress)
Evergreen conifer – 1 plant
Tall, columnar conifer with dark blue foliage. H 4–5m (13–16ft); S 1m (3ft 3in).

7 Skimmia japonica 'Foremanii'
Evergreen shrub – 1 plant
Leaves oval, glossy. Flowerheads off-white, borne in spring; sometimes followed by red berries. H 1.2m (4ft); S 1m (3ft 3in).

8 Berberis thunbergii 'Rose Glow' (barberry)
Deciduous shrub – 1 plant
Foliage purple variegated pink. H 1.8m (6ft); S 1.8m (6 ft).

9 Clematis armandii
Evergreen climber – 1 plant
Leaves mid-green, glossy. Small, white, fragrant flowers produced in early summer. Requires training. H 3m (10ft); S 3m (10ft).

10 Choisya ternata 'Sundance' (Mexican orange blossom)
Evergreen shrub – 1 plant
Foliage bright yellow, fading to lime-green in deep shade. White flowers in late spring, often again in autumn. Susceptible to frost damage. H 1.5m (5ft); S 1.5m (5ft).

11 Garrya elliptica (silk-tassel bush)
Evergreen shrub – 1 plant
Very dark, matt foliage. Pale green catkins in spring. Can be wall-trained. H 3m (10ft); S 1.2m (4ft).

12 Heuchera micrantha 'Palace Purple' (alum root)
Semi-evergreen herbaceous – 3 plants
Leaves bold, deeply cut, purple. Off-white flowerheads in summer. H 30cm (12in); S 30cm (12in).

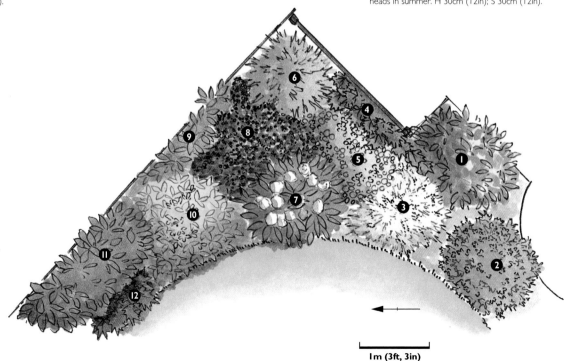

1m (3ft, 3in)

MIXED SHADY PLANTING

These borders, found in the plan on page 89 are, for much of the time, in shade and the plants have been selected accordingly. The soil is medium loam with a neutral pH and seldom dries out completely.

1 **Jasminum nudiflorum (winter jasmine)**
Deciduous climber – 1 plant
Flowers bright yellow, appear in winter and early spring. Training required. H 2m (6ft 6in); S 2m (6ft 6in).

2 **Iris foetidissima (Gladwin, stinking Iris)**
Evergreen herbaceous – 1–3plants
Foliage strap-shaped. Greenish flowers borne in early summer. Orange-red, fleshy seeds. H 60cm (2ft); S 45cm (18in).

3 **Euphorbia characias ssp. wulfenii (syn. E. wulfenii) (milkweed, Spurge)**
Semi-evergreen herbaceous – 2–3 plants
Leaves bluish grey. Flowers greenish, produced in early summer. Sap poisonous. H 90cm (3ft); S 30cm (12in).

4 **Spiraea japonica 'Goldflame' (syn. S. bumalda 'Gold Flame')**
Deciduous shrub – 1 plant
Foliage golden. Purple-pink flowers appear in summer. H 1.2m (4ft); S 90cm (3ft).

5 **Pyracantha 'Orange Glow' (firethorn)**
Evergreen shrub – 1 plant
Thorny. Flowers off-white, produced in spring; orange-red berries. Can be wall-trained or left unpruned. H 3m (10ft); S 2m (6ft 6in); can be kept within 50cm (20in) deep.

6 **Liriope muscari (lilyturf)**
Semi-evergreen herbaceous – 3 plants
Leaves grassy, evergreen. Flowers in summer; mauve and berry-like. H 30cm (12in); S 20cm (8in).

7 **Euonymus fortunei 'Emerald Gaiety'**
Evergreen shrub – 1 to 2 plants
Ground cover, but will clamber. Leaves variegated white and green. H (unsupported) 25cm (9in); s 75 cm (2ft 6in).

8 **Hydrangea macrophylla (mophead hydrangea)**
Deciduous shrub – 1 plant
Leaves oval, toothed. Flowers in mid- to late summer; pink to blue depending on cultivar and soil pH; also white available. H 1.5m (5ft); S 1.5m (5ft).

9 **Hedera colcicha 'Dentata Aurea' (Persian ivy)**
Evergreen climber – 1 plant
Rampant. Leaves large, green and cream variegation. H 3m (10ft); S 3m (10ft).

10 **Arundinaria viridistriata (Bamboo) (syn. Pleioblastus auricomus)**
Evergreen bamboo – 1 to 3 plants
Leaves brightly striped yellow and green. H 1.2m (4ft); S 50cm (20in).

11 **Hebe pinguifolia 'Pagei' (disk-leaved Hebe)**
Evergreen sub-shrub – 1 to 2 plants
Foliage blue-grey. Flowers white, borne in summer. H 20cm (8in); S 45cm (18in).

12 **Viburnum davidii**
Evergreen shrub – 1 plant
Leaves deeply veined and glossy. Small, white flowers in summer, followed by blue-grey berries. H 1.5m (5 ft); S 1.5m (5ft).

13 **Euonymus japonicus 'Aureopictus' (Japanese spindle)**
Evergreen shrub – 1 plant
Foliage variegated green and gold. H 1.8m (6ft); s 1.2m (4ft).

14 **Helleborus argutifolius (syn. H. corsicus) (Christmas rose, Lenten rose, hellebore)**
Semi-evergreen herbaceous – 1 to 2 plants
Bold foliage. Spring-flowering; blooms pale apple-green in colour. H 60cm (2ft); S 60cm (2ft).

15 **Fuchsia 'Mrs Popple'**
Deciduous shrub – 1 plant
Red and purple flowers in mid-summer. Susceptible to frost damage. H 1.2m (4ft); S 1.2m (4ft).

16 **Chaenomeles speciosa 'Brilliant' (flowering quince)**
Deciduous shrub – 1 plant
Best as wall plant. Flowers scarlet in early spring. Fruit small, yellowish. H 2m (6ft 6in); S 3m (10ft).

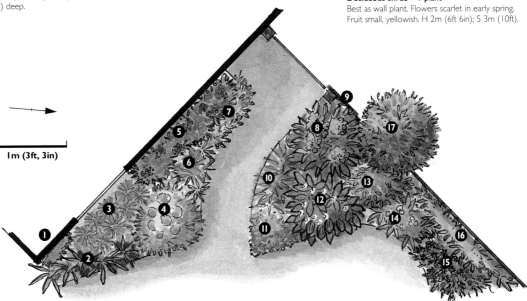

1m (3ft, 3in)

PLANTING UNDER TREES

This planting plan is from the design on page 51. Since the ground under trees is often dry as well as shady, add plenty of well-rotted manure or humus prior to planting. Feed and water new plants until well established.

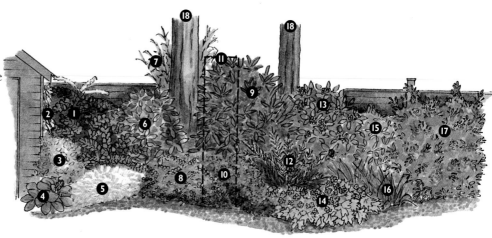

1 Mahonia x media 'Charity'
Evergreen shrub – 1 plant
Foliage glossy and slightly spiny. Flowers fragrant and yellow, produced in winter and early spring. H 3m (10ft); S 1.8m (6ft).

2 Hedera colchica 'Sulphur Heart' (syn. H. c. 'Paddy's Pride') (Persian ivy)
Evergreen climber – 1 plant
Vigorous. Leaves large, dark green with bold central splash of yellow. H 3m (10ft); S 1.8m (6ft).

3 Kerria japonica 'Picta' (syn. K. j. variegata)
Deciduous shrub – 1 plant
Leaves variegated white and green. Single yellow flowers in spring. H 1m (3ft 3in); S 60cm (2ft).

4 Bergenia cordifolia
Evergreen herbaceous – 3 to 5 plants
Leaves large and evergreen. Flowers white and pale to deep pink, produced in early spring. H 40cm (16in); S 45cm (18in).

5 Senecio 'Sunshine' (Brachyglottis Dunedin Hybrid Group 'Sunshine')
Evergreen shrub – 1 plant
Foliage silver-grey. Flowers yellow, produced in summer. H 90cm (3ft); S 1.5m (5ft).

6 Aucuba japonica 'Picturata' (Japanese laurel)
Evergreen shrub – 1 plant
Leaves variegated with central splash of yellow. H 1.8m (6ft); S 1.8m (6ft).

7 Arundinaria murieliae (syn. Fargesia murieliae) (muriel bamboo)
Evergreen bamboo – 1 plant
Leaves small. May be slow to establish initially. H 3m (10ft); S 1.5m (5ft).

8 Symphoricarpos x chenaultii 'Hancock'
Deciduous shrub – 1 plant
Green leaves on weeping branches. H 1.2m (4ft); S 1.5m (5ft).

9 Photinia x fraseri 'Red Robin'
Evergreen shrub – 1 plant
Foliage bright red when young, ageing bronze-red then green. H 3m (10ft); S 1.8m (6ft).

10 Buxus sempervirens 'Aureovariegata' (common box)
Evergreen shrub – 1 plant
Leaves dark green, striped or mottled creamy-yellow. H 1.5m (5ft); S 1.5m (5ft).

11 Lonicera periclymenum 'Belgica' (common honeysuckle, woodbine)
Deciduous climber – 1 plant
Flowers borne in mid-summer, pale rose and yellow in colour; highly fragrant. H 3m (10ft); S 1.5m (5ft).

12 Athyrium filix-femina 'Vernoniae' (lady fern)
Deciduous fern – 1 plant
Fronds strong-growing if given humus-rich soil. H 90cm (3ft); S 60cm (2ft).

13 Cotoneaster lacteus
Evergreen shrub – 1 plant
Leaves leathery. Flowers white, in summer; berries red, in autumn or winter. H 2.4m (8ft); S 2.4m (8ft).

14 Geranium 'Johnson's Blue' (cranesbill)
Semi-evergreen herbaceous – 3 plants
Leaves deeply divided, mid-green. Flowers clear blue, from mid- to late summer. H 30cm (12in); s 40cm (16in).

15 Euonymus japonicus 'Albomarginatus' (Japanese spindle)
Evergreen shrub – 1 to 3 plants
Leaves green with white margins. H 1.8m (6ft); s 1–1.2m (3ft 3–4in).

16 Helictotrichon sempervirens (syn. Avena candida) (blue oat grass)
Evergreen grass – 1 to 3 plants
Foliage steel-blue. Straw-coloured flowers in early summer. H 30cm (12in); S 30cm (12in).

17 Pyracantha 'Golden Charmer' (firethorn)
Evergreen shrub – 1 plant
Thorny. Leaves glossy. Flowers white, borne in early summer; gold-coloured berries in early autumn. H 3m (10ft); S 2m (6ft 6in).

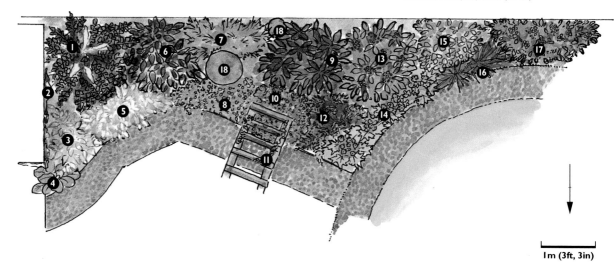

1m (3ft, 3in)

LOW SHADY PLANTING

This planting, from the design on page 54, is suitable for any narrow border where a low planting is required. The soil is moist and slightly acid, and many of the plants require a high humus content.

1 *Rhododendron* **'Elizabeth'**
Evergreen shrub – 1 plant
Leaves dark green and medium-sized. Flowers scarlet, in spring. H 1.2m (4ft); S 1.2m (4ft).

2 *Hebe* **'Mrs Winder'**
Evergreen shrub – 1 plant
Foliage purple-bronze. Flowers bright blue, in summer. Reasonably hardy but susceptible to wind scorch in winter. H 60cm (2ft); S 60cm (2ft).

3 *Vinca minor* **'Variegata' (syn. *V. m.* 'Argentovariegata') (lesser periwinkle)**
Evergreen sub-shrub – 1 plant
Ground cover. Leaves small, green and cream variegated. Flowers blue, borne in early summer. H 20cm (8in); S 75cm (2ft 6in).

4 *Hosta undulata* var. *albomarginata* (syn. *H.* 'Thomas Hogg') or *H.* 'Ground Master' (plantain lily)
Herbaceous – 1 or 3 plants respectively
Leaves white and green variegated; flowers mid-summer. Both die back to crown each winter and require protection from slugs and snails in spring and summer. *H. u. albomarginata*: mauve flowers; H 50cm (20in); S 50cm (20in). *H.* 'Ground Master': violet-purple flowers; H 30cm (12in); S 30cm (12in).

5 *Ophiopogon planiscapus* **'Nigrescens' (black grass)**
Evergreen grass – 1–3 plants
Leaves black, grassy in spreading clumps. H 20cm (8in); S 25cm (10in).

6 *Lamium maculatum* **'White Nancy' (deadnettle)**
Semi-evergreen herbaceous – 1 to 3 plants
Ground cover; growth spreading, almost prostrate. Leaves nettle-shaped, bright silver. Flowers white, produced from late spring to summer. H 10cm (4in); S 40cm (16in).

7 *Epimedium perralderianum*
Semi-evergreen herbaceous – 1 plant
Ground cover. Leaves heart-shaped; good autumn colour; Flowers bronze-yellow, appear from late spring to early summer. H 30cm (12in); S 30cm (12in).

8 *Adiantum pedatum* **(northern maidenhair fern)**
Semi-evergreen fern – 3 plants
Foliage fresh green; fine, dark stems. H 20cm (8in) S 30cm (12in).

9 *Pachysandra terminalis* **'Variegata'**
Evergreen shrub – 1 plant
Spreads to form ground cover. Leaves cream and green variegated. H 20cm (8in); S 30cm (12in).

10 *Hebe* **'Youngii' (syn. *H.* 'Carl Teschner')**
Evergreen shrub – 1 to 3 plants
Moderately hardy. Leaves dark green-purple. Violet-white flowers produced in summer. H 25cm (10in); S 30cm (12in).

11 *Viola riviniana* (syn. *V. labradorica* **Purpurea Group) (violet)**
Semi-evergreen herbaceous – 3 plants
Foliage bold, purplish-green; spreads to form ground cover. Light blue flowers appear in spring. H 10cm (4in); S 15cm (6in).

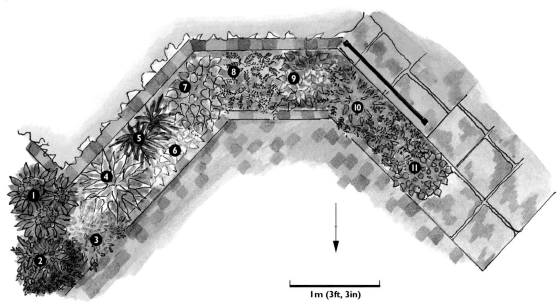

1m (3ft, 3in)

MIXED PLANTING FOR RAISED BED

This plan features in the garden design on page 33. The plants will grow in any sunny, sheltered, raised bed with well-drained, neutral soil. Make sure there is support for climbing plants.

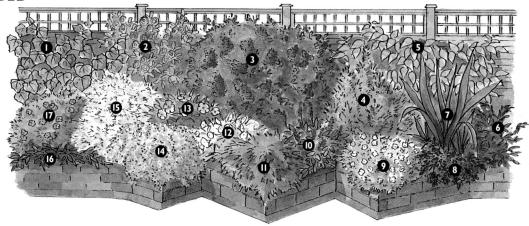

1 **Vitis coignetiae (crimson glory vine)**
Deciduous climber – 1 plant
Vigorous. Leaves large, colouring in autumn. Tie in regularly. H 2m (6ft 6in); S 2m (6ft 6in).

2 **Rosa 'Maigold' (climbing rose)**
Deciduous climber – 1 plant
Foliage glossy green. Flowers in summer; semi-double, golden-yellow and scented. Train along wires. H 2–3m (6ft 6in–10ft); S 2–3m (6ft 6in–10ft).

3 **Ceanothus dentatus**
Evergreen shrub – 1 plant
Rich blue flowers from late spring to early summer. Not always hardy. H 2.4m (8ft); S 2.4m (8ft).

4 **Rosmarinus officinalis 'Miss Jessopp's Upright' (syn. R. o. 'Miss Jessop') (rosemary)**
Evergreen shrubby herb – 1 plant
Upright habit. Foliage grey-green, needle-like. Flowers blue, borne in late spring. H 1.2–1.8m (4–6ft); S 60cm–1.2m (2–4ft).

5 **Actinidia kolomikta**
Deciduous climber – 1 plant
Reasonably vigorous. Heart-shaped leaves; pink patches at tips. Train along wires. H 3m (10ft); S 3m (10ft).

6 **Euphorbia amygdaloïdes 'Rubra' (wood spurge)**
Evergreen or semi-evergreen herbaceous – 3 plants
Foliage red and maroon. Greenish flowers produced in summer. Sap poisonous. H 60cm (2ft); S 30cm (12in).

7 **Phormium tenax 'Purpureum' (New Zealand flax)**
Evergreen – 1 plant
Architectural, purple, strap-shaped leaves. Requires shelter. H 1.5m (5ft); S 1m (3ft 3in).

8 **Cotoneaster dammeri var. radicans (syn. C. d. 'Radicans')**
Evergreen sub-shrub – 1 to 2 plants
Small, glossy, dark green leaves. White flowers in summer; red berries in autumn. H 15cm (6in); S 1.2m (4ft).

9 **Potentilla fruticosa var. mandshurica (syn. P. f. 'Mandschurica')**
Deciduous shrub – 1 plant
Greyish foliage. Small, white flowers from late summer to early autumn. H 25cm (9in); S 1m (3ft 3in).

10 **Salvia officinalis 'Purpurascens' (sage)**
Semi-evergreen shrubby herb – 1 plant
Leaves green to soft purple. Flower spikes purple-blue, from summer to autumn. H 60cm (2ft); S 60–75cm (2–2ft 6in).

11 **Juniperus squamata 'Blue Carpet' (flaky juniper)**
Evergreen conifer – 1 plant
Prostrate conifer. Foliage silvery-blue. H 30cm (12in); S 1–1.2m (3ft 3in–4ft).

12 **Convolvulus cneorum**
Semi-evergreen shrub – 1 plant in sunny sites; 2 to 3 in cool, exposed areas
Foliage silvery-white. Flowers white, trumpet-shaped, borne from late spring to late summer. Susceptible to frost damage. H 60cm (2ft); S 75cm (2ft 6in).

13 **Cistus 'Silver Pink' (rock rose)**
Evergreen shrub – 1 plant
Rounded. Leaves slightly felted. Silky pink flowers produced from early to mid-summer. Susceptible to winter damage. H 75cm (2ft 6in); S 75cm (2ft 6in).

14 **Cotoneaster atropurpureus 'Variegatus' (syn. C. horizontalis variegata)**
Semi-evergreen shrub – 1 plant
Weeping habit. Foliage variegated. White flowers produced from spring to summer, followed by bright red berries. H 30cm (12in); S 1m (3ft 3in).

15 **Artemisia 'Powis Castle' (syn. A. arborescens 'Powis Castle') (wormwood)**
Semi-evergreen shrubby herb – 1 plant
Foliage aromatic, silvery-green, feathery. H 90cm (3ft); S 90cm (3ft).

16 **Ajuga reptans 'Braunherz'**
Semi-evergreen herbaceous – 1 to 2 plants
Rosettes of glossy, purple leaves forming ground cover. Blue flower spikes appear in summer. H 10cm (4in); S 60-75cm (2–2ft 6in).

17 **Potentilla fruticosa 'Sunset'**
Deciduous shrub – 1 plant
Tiny, greyish leaves. Orange-red flowers appear in summer. H 45cm (18in); S 1.2m (4ft).

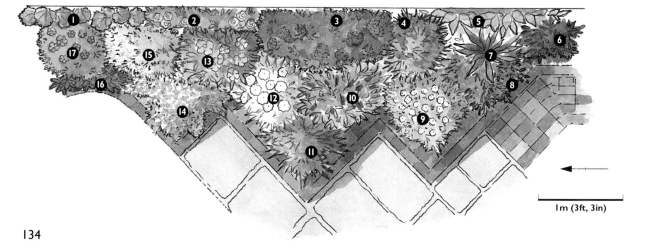

1m (3ft, 3in)

SCREE BED

This planting is from the design on page 85, but the plants will grow in any well-drained site: cover a layer of stones with gritty compost (neutral to alkaline), and top with rocks. The bed will need protection from winter rain.

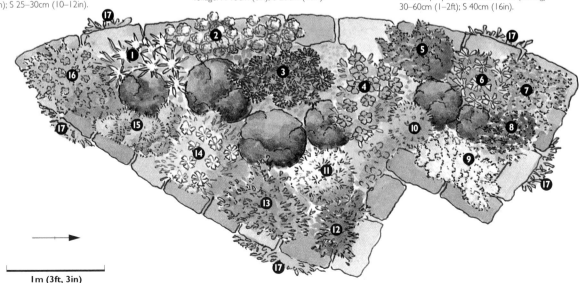

1 **Leontopodium alpinum (edelweiss)**
Evergreen or semi-evergreen alpine – 1 to 3 plants
Leaves greyish-green; lemon-scented. White flowers in mid-summer. H 25cm (10in); S 25cm (10in).

2 **Sedum spathulifolium 'Cape blanco' (stonecrop)**
Evergreen alpine – 1 to 3 plants
Single rosettes of silvery-grey, succulent leaves. Flowers yellow, appear in summer. H 10cm (4in); S 15–20cm (6–8in).

3 **Sempervivum tectorum 'Triste' (common houseleek)**
Evergreen alpine – 1 to 3 plants
Bronze, fleshy leaves held in tight, spreading clusters. Flowers pinkish, borne in summer. H 15cm (6in); S 15cm (6in).

4 **Helianthemum 'Rhodanthe Carneum' (syn. H. 'Wisley Pink') (rock rose)**
Semi-evergreen sub-shrub – 1 plant
Rather sparse. Leaves greyish-green. Flowers soft pink, in summer. H 30cm (12in); S 30cm (12in).

5 **Thymus serpyllum coccineus (syn. T. s. 'Coccineus') (thyme)**
Semi-evergreen alpine – 1 to 3 plants
Prostrate, mat-forming shrub with tiny, dark leaves. Purple-red flowers produced in summer. H 2.5cm (1in); S 25–30cm (10–12in).

6 **Hypericum polyphyllum 'Grandiflorum'**
Semi-evergreen sub-shrub – 1 plant
Yellow, showy flowers produced in summer. H 15cm (6in); S 15cm (6in).

7 **Thymus 'Doone Valley' (thyme)**
Semi-evergreen alpine – 1 plant
Spreading, prostrate. Tiny green and yellow variegated leaves. H 2.5cm (1in); S 15cm (6in).

8 **Dianthus deltoides 'Flashing Light' (maiden pink)**
Semi-evergreen alpine – 3 to 5 plants
Dark, mat-forming foliage. Tiny, red, single flowers in summer. H 10cm (4in); S 7–10cm (2¾–4in).

9 **Raoulia australis**
Semi-evergreen alpine – 1 to 3 plants
Spreading prostrate mats of tiny, silvery-grey leaves. Requires protection from winter wet. H 1.5cm (⅛in); S 15cm (6in).

10 **Vitaliana primuliflora (syn. Douglasia vitaliana)**
Evergreen alpine – 1 to 3 plants
Hummocks of green foliage. Stemless yellow flowers in spring. H 4cm (1½in); S 10cm (4in).

11 **Artemisia schmidtiana 'Nana' (wormwood)**
Evergreen alpine – 1 to 3 plants
Tiny rosettes of silvery-grey, aromatic, needle-like foliage. H 15cm (6in); S 25cm (10in).

12 **Sedum cauticola 'Lidakense' (syn. S. lidakense) (stonecrop)**
Semi-evergreen alpine – 1 plant
Low, spreading, greyish-green, succulent foliage. Flowers deep pink, produced in summer. Slightly invasive. H 10cm (4¼in); S (trailing) 20cm (8in).

13 **Veronica prostrata (prostrate speedwell)**
Semi-evergreen herbaceous – 1 to 2 plants
Prostrate. Foliage light green. Flowers clear blue, in early summer. H 15cm (6in); S 25cm (10in).

14 **Arenaria montana (sandwort)**
Semi-evergreen alpine – 1 plant
Mat-forming, greyish-green foliage. White flowers appear in mid-summer. H 10cm (4in); S 20cm (8in).

15 **Arenaria balearica (sandwort)**
Herbaceous – 1 to 3 plants
Mat-forming leaves; tiny and emerald-green. Flowers small and white, produced from late spring to early summer. H 5cm (2in); S 15cm (6in).

16 **Frankenia thymifolia**
Semi-evergreen alpine – 1 plant
Mat-forming, soft green foliage. Small, pink flowers borne in mid-summer. H 5cm (2in); S 25cm (10in).

17 **Aubrieta**
Semi-evergreen alpine – 3 or more plants
Foliage trailing. Flowers profusely in spring; most varieties purple-blue in colour. H: (trailing) 30–60cm (1–2ft); S 40cm (16in).

1m (3ft, 3in)

HERBACEOUS COTTAGE BORDER

This planting, from the design on page 77, will suit any sunny border with a sheltered yet fairly open aspect and light, well-drained, slightly alkaline soil. The herbaceous plants may die down in winter, but the evergreens provide winter interest.

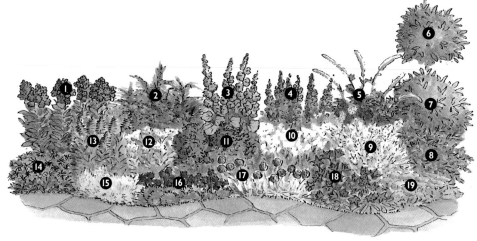

1 *Phlox* **'Sandringham'**
Herbaceous – 3 plants
Flowers cyclamen-pink, produced from mid- to late summer. H 75cm (2ft 6in); S 30cm (12in).

2 *Foeniculum vulgare* **'Purpureum' (purple fennel)**
Herbaceous – 1 to 3 plants
Foliage feathery, dark purple fronds. Umbels of yellow flowers in summer. H 1.8m (6ft); S 50cm (20in).

3 *Alcea rosea* **cultivars (syn.** *Althaea rosea***) (hollyhock)**
Herbaceous – 3 plants
Upright spikes of funnel-shaped flowers borne in summer: cream, pink, apricot or red; single or double. H 2.4m (8ft); S 50cm (20in).

4 *Sidalcea* **'Rose Queen'**
Herbaceous – 3 plants
Flowers silky-pink, mallow-shaped, from mid-summer onwards. H 1.2m (4ft); S 30cm (12in).

5 *Cimicifuga simplex* **'Brunette' (syn.** *C. ramosa* **'Brunette') (bugbane)**
Herbaceous – 1 plant
Foliage deep purple, elder-shaped. White, cats'-tail-like flowerheads in late summer. H 1.8m (6ft); S 75cm (2ft 6in).

6 *Prunus* **x** *sargentii* **(sargent cherry)**
Deciduous tree – 1 plant
Leaves coppery-red fading to green for summer, colouring well for autumn. Single, pink flowers in spring. H 5–6m (16–20ft); S 1.8–2.4m (6–8ft).

7 *Elaeagnus* **x** *ebbingei*
Evergreen shrub – 1 plant
Foliage greyish-green. H 3m (10ft); S 2.4m (8ft) but can be pruned back.

8 *Abelia* **x** *grandiflora*
Semi-evergreen shrub – 1 plant
Habit slightly weeping. Leaves green, tinged red. Flowers pink, appear from late summer to early autumn. H 1.2m (4ft); S 1.2m (4ft).

9 *Helichrysum serotinum* **(syn.** *H. angustifolium***) (curry plant)**
Semi-evergreen shrub – 1 plant
Foliage silvery, aromatic. Yellow flowers in summer, but usually removed. H 90cm (3ft); S 60cm (2ft).

10 *Achillea ptarmica* **'The Pearl' (batchelor's buttons)**
Herbaceous – 1 to 3 plants
Foliage bright green. Flowers small white 'buttons', in late summer. H 75cm (2ft 6in); S 30cm (12in).

11 *Campanula lactiflora* **(bellflower)**
Herbaceous – 1 to 3 plants
Flowers lavender-blue, produced in mid-summer. H 90cm (3ft); S 40cm (16in).

12 *Anaphalis triplinervis* **(pearl everlasting)**
Semi-evergreen herbaceous – 3 plants
Foliage greyish-white. White, papery flowers borne in late summer. H 60cm (2ft); S 30cm (12in).

13 *Physostegia virginiana* **'Bouquet Rose ' (obedient plant)**
Herbaceous – 3 plants
Foliage bright green. Pink, tubular flowers in late summer. H 75cm (2ft 6in); S 30cm (12in).

14 *Aster thomsonii* **'Nanus' (Michaelmas daisy)**
Herbaceous – 3 plants
Foliage grey-green. Lavender-blue flowers, mid-summer to autumn. H 45cm (18in); S 30cm (12in).

15 *Artemisia pontica* **(Roman wormwood)**
Herbaceous – 3 plants
Foliage feathery, silver-grey and aromatic. H 25cm (10in); S 40cm (16in).

16 *Armeria maritima* **'Ruby glow' (sea pink, thrift)**
Evergreen herbaceous – 3 plants
Evergreen foliage forms clumps. Pompom flowers small and deep pink, from mid-summer to autumn. H 25cm (10in); S 25cm (10in).

17 *Dianthus* **'Doris' (garden pink)**
Semi-evergreen herbaceous – 3 to 5 plants
Semi-evergreen, grass-like, grey leaves . Flowers pink and scented, from mid-summer onwards. H 30cm (12in); S 20cm (8in).

18 *Platycodon grandiflorus mariesii*
Herbaceous – 3 plants
Flowers deep blue and cup-shaped, produced in late summer. H 45cm (18in); S 25cm (10in).

19 *Solidago* **'Golden Thumb' (syn.** *S.* **'Queenie') (dwarf golden rod)**
Herbaceous – 3 plants
Yellow plumes of flowers produced in late summer. H 30cm (12in); S 30cm (12in).

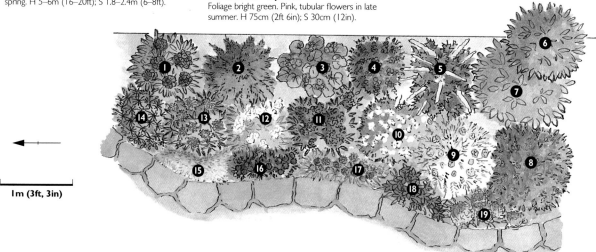

1m (3ft, 3in)

BOG GARDEN

Here is a plan for a partially shaded, damp bed adjacent to a small pool, as seen in the design on page 30. Most of these plants need moist soil in which to grow.

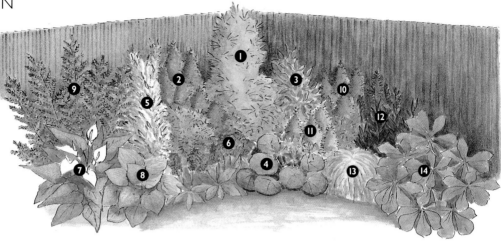

1 *Fargesia murieliae* **'Simba' (syn.** *Arundinaria murieliae* **'Simba') (muriel bamboo)**
   Evergreen bamboo – 1 plant
   Habit compact. Leaves small and bright green. H 1.8m (6ft); S 1.2m (4ft).

2 *Astilbe* **'Bressingham Beauty'**
   Herbaceous – 1 plant
   Spikes of plume-like, rich pink flowers, from mid- to late summer. H 90cm (3ft); S 75cm (2ft 6in).

3 *Cornus alba* **'Spaethii' (red-barked dogwood)**
   Deciduous shrub – 1 plant
   Shrub with distinctive dark red stems for winter display; bright yellow and green variegated foliage. If pruned annually: H 1.2m (4 ft); S. 1.2m (4ft).

4 *Ligularia dentata* **'Desdemona' (syn.** *L. clivorum* **'Desdemona')**
   Herbaceous – 1 plant
   Foliage bold, purplish-green; flowers contrasting yellow-orange, produced in summer. H 60–90cm (2–3ft); S. 60–75cm (2–2ft 6in).

5 *Salix integra* **'Hakuro-nishiki' (syn.** *S. i.* **'Albo-maculata' (variegated shrubby willow)**
   Deciduous shrub – 1 plant
   Foliage densely variegated off-white; new shoots often pink. If pruned annually: H 90cm (3ft); S 1–1.2m (3ft 3in–4ft).

6 *Primula pulverulenta* **(candelabra primula)**
   Semi-evergreen herbaceous – 3 plants
   Foliage bright green. Flowers rosy-red borne in tiers, from early to mid-summer. H 45cm (18in); S. 25cm (10in).

7 *Zantedeschia aethiopica* **'Crowborough' (arum lily)**
   Herbaceous – 1 plant
   Foliage bold, dark green; flowers pure white borne from mid- to late summer. Crown needs winter protection. H 90cm (3ft); S. 60cm (2ft).

8 *Hosta fortunei* **(plantain lily)**
   Herbaceous – 1 plant
   Bold, glaucous, heart-shaped foliage. Highly susceptible to slug damage. H 75cm (2ft 6in); S. 60cm (2ft).

9 *Osmunda regalis* **(regal fern)**
   Semi-evergreen fern – 1 plant
   Fresh green fronds in summer, turning rich brown in autumn, dying back to fibrous crown. Dislikes chalk. H 1.2m (4ft); S 1–1.2m (3ft 3in–4ft).

10 *Astilbe* **'Superba'**
   Herbaceous – 1 to 3 plants
   Rosy-purple flower spikes in mid-summer. Grow in well-manured soil. H 1.2m (4ft); S. 40cm (16in).

11 *Astilbe* **'Rheinland'**
   Herbaceous – 3 plants
   Flower spikes rich pink, produced in mid-summer. H 50cm (20in); S. 40cm (16in).

12 *Lobelia* **'Queen Victoria' (cardinal flower)**
   Herbaceous – 3 plants
   Foliage shiny and purplish-maroon. Scarlet flower spikes produced in summer. Highly susceptible to slug damage. H 90cm (3ft); S 30cm (12in).

13 *Hakonechloa macra* **'Alboaurea' (Japanese grass)**
   Evergreen grass – 1 plant
   Grass with weeping foliage, variegated gold and green. Clump forming. H 25cm (10in); S 30cm (12in).

14 *Rodgersia pinnata* **'Elegans'**
   Herbaceous – 1 plant
   Bronze-tinged, horse-chestnut-shaped leaves. Flower plumes off-white, from late spring to early summer. H 90cm (3ft); S 60–75cm (2–2ft 6in).

1m (3ft, 3in)

A

Acid Describes soils with pH of less than 7.0.

Aggregate Gravel or small pebbles mixed with cement.

Alkaline Describes soils with pH of more than 7.0.

Annual Plant completing its life-cycle from seed to seed in one season.

Arris rail Wooden rail, triangular in profile, running parallel to the ground and supported between uprights, to which boards are fixed to form a fence.

Aspect The direction in which a garden faces. This has an influence on the choice of design and plants as it will determine which areas of the garden are in sun and which are in shade at various times of day.

B

Back-fill To place soil, aggregate or a similar material in a hole to support a plant or post inserted into it.

Bare-rooted Describes plants lifted from nursery beds with little or no soil attached to the roots.

Batter Inward slope of a hedge or stone wall to ensure that the top is narrower than the bottom.

C

Canopy Cover and, more often than not, shade provided by the branches of trees.

Catkin Hanging spike of tiny flowers.

Cement Powdered limestone and clay used to make mortar or concrete.

Columnar Describes upright, column-like growth of a plant (usually a tree or shrub).

Compost Potting medium, or material made of decomposed plant remains.

Concrete Mix of sand, cement, aggregate and water which forms hard building material when dry.

Coniferous Plant, usually evergreen, that bears cones.

Container-grown Describes plant raised and sold in a pot, as opposed to bare-rooted.

Cross-fall Slight slope incorporated into the construction of an area of paving or hard surfacing which allows water to drain off it in an appropriate direction.

Cultivar Cultivated variety.

Cure To assist in the hardening of concrete by keeping it moist.

Cuttings Parts of a plant cut off to be used for propagating other plants with identical characteristics.

D

Deciduous Describes a plant that loses all its leaves, usually in autumn.

Division Method of propagating a plant by splitting it into small portions for replanting.

Dormant Describes the resting period, usually winter, when plants make little or no growth.

Double A flower which has multiple rows of petals.

E

English bond Method of laying bricks in a specific pattern.

Expansion joint A break in the bond of a wall running the full height, possibly filled with expanded polystyrene concealed with a weak mortar pointing. This is intended to allow for seasonal expansion or contraction yet prevent the masonry from cracking.

Engineering brick Particularly hard brick suitable for paving.

Ericaceous When applied to compost, suitable for lime-hating plants.

Evergreen Describes a plant that retains its leaves all year.

F

Fall See cross-fall.

Fastigiate Describes a tree or shrub, the branches of which grow almost vertically.

Flemish bond Method of laying bricks in a specific pattern.

Flettons A type of brick, too soft for paving material.

Framework Permanent, trained structure of shoots or branches.

Free-standing Growing without support.

Fronds Leaf-like part of a fern.

G

Germination Development of seed into seedlings.

Glaucous Describes usually leaves with a blue-green, grey or white bloom.

Gravel board Horizontal strip of timber attached to the bottom of a fence.

Grout Mortar filling between bricks.

H

Habit Natural style of growth and shape of a plant.

Half-hardy Describes a plant that cannot survive winter conditions without some protection.

Hardcore Foundation material made of broken-up pieces of brick.

Hardy Describes a plant that can survive winter conditions without protection.

Haunching Strip of mortar laid alongside edging bricks to provide support.

Head Describes height to which water will be raised by a pump.

Herbaceous Describes non-woody plants the upper parts of which die down to the rootstock at the end of the growing season and remain dormant during winter.

Herbicide A chemical used for the control of weeds.

Hoggin Mix of sand and gravel.

Humus Semi-decomposed organic matter.

Hybrid Plant derived by crossing two distinct species or varieties.

J

Joist A supporting beam.

Juvenile Describes young type of growth.

L

Leaf mould Decomposed leaves.

Loam Type of soil, usually quite fertile, containing clay, silt and sand and is usually rich in humus.

M

Medium A compost growing mixture or other material in which plants may be grown or propagated.

Mortar Mix of cement, lime, sand and water used between bricks.

Mulch Material spread over soil surface.

N

Naturalized Describes plants grown as if in the wild.

Neutral Describes soil with a pH of 7, which is neither acid nor alkaline.

O

Organic matter Mulches, composts etc based on decomposed plant matter.

P

Paviors Paving blocks in a variety of sizes and colours.

Perennial Plant that survives more than three seasons.

pH Measurement of soil acidity. pH7 is said to be neutral, above is alkaline, below is acid.

Perspective trellis A flat wall-mounted trellis incorporating a tunnel effect which is used to give an illusion of space.

Piers Supporting column built into a brick wall.

Plumb line Weight attached to string to indicate vertical.

Pointing Technique of finishing off joints between bricks with mortar.

Post cap Protective piece attached to the top of a wooden upright.

Pruning Systematic removal of dead, diseased or unwanted woody stems.

Prostrate Describes a habit in which growth is almost horizontal.

R

Riser Vertical face of a step.

Rootstock Plant providing roots for another plant of the same variety, which is grafted on to it.

Rosette Circular cluster of leaves.

Running bond Method of laying bricks in a specific pattern.

S

Sap Juice of a plant.

Scarify Spring and autumn treatment for lawns which consists of vigorously raking up thatch and moss.

Scree A slope made up of rock fragments, sometimes used in rock gardens.

Semi-evergreen Describes a plant that loses only some of its leaves during the year.

Sett Paving block usually made of granite.

Shrub Woody plant with several branches originating at or near the base.

Single Describes a flower with a single layer of petals.

Soakaway A pit filled with gravel into which excess soil water can drain.

Species Category in botanical classification, directly below genus, containing closely related, similar plants.

Spike Describes a stem of stalkless flowers.

Stretcher bond Method of laying bricks in a specific pattern.

Sub-shrub A plant with herbaceous tips and a woody base.

Subsoil Layer of soil below topsoil, lighter in colour and less fertile.

Succulent Describes a plant with thick, fleshy leaves.

Systemic Describes a chemical (usually pesticide or herbicide) that is carried through the plant after application.

T

Tamp To pack down soil or concrete, for example.

Tread Horizontal part of a step.

V

Varieties Naturally occurring variants of a species.

Variegated Describes leaves with coloured markings.

W

Weep-holes Vertical joints in a retaining wall left free of mortar to allow drainage of water.

Weeping Describes a habit, usually of trees and shrubs in which terminal growth droops downwards.

Photographic acknowledgments

Amateur Gardening 20 bottom, 25 right, 26, 28 bottom, 29 bottom left, 29 top right, 29 bottom right, 32 bottom, 35 top right, 35 bottom right, 35 centre right, 43, 44 bottom, 44 centre, 46 top, 47 right, 49 right, 51 bottom, 53 bottom, 53 centre top, 53 top, 53 centre bottom, 56 left, 58 bottom, 61 right, 63, 65 centre right, 65 bottom right, 70 top right, 70 top left, 73 top, 74 bottom right, 75 bottom, 75 centre, 79 top right, 79 centre right, 79 bottom, 81 bottom, 83 right, 89 bottom, **Kingston Maurward College, Dorset** 28 centre; **Jerry Harpur/ Christopher Masson** 6/7; **Andrew Lawson** 16/17; **Marianne Majerus** 66/67; **Reed International Books Ltd/Michael Boys** 19, 20 above, 22, 23 below left, 25 left, 27, 28 top, 31, 32 above, 34 below, 34 above, 35 below left, 40, 41 below right, 41 above right, 41 left, 44 top, 45 top, 45 centre, 45 bottom, 46 below left, 46 below right, 47 left, 50, 52, 53 left, 56 right, 57, 58 centre left, 58 top left, 59 above, 59 below, 62, 64 above, 64 below, 64, 65 top left, 65 top right, 69 below left, 70 below, 71 above right, 71 below right, 74 below left, 74 top, 75 top right, 78 below, 78 above, 79 above left, 82, 83 below left, 86 above, 86 below, 87 below, 87 centre, 87 above, 90, 91 above, 91 below, 92/3, 124.